AF390198

SHIBBOLETH

SHIBBOLETH
A TEMPLAR MONITOR

by
Sir George Cooper Connor

MASONICA
Publishers of the Ancient Craft

Shibboleth
SIR GEORGE COOPER CONNOR

Fifth Edition
Nashville, Tennessee
Order of the Red Cross
[1894]

MASONICA®
Publishers of the Ancient Craft
www.freemasonrybooks.com

© 2021 ENTREACACIAS, S.L.

ENTREACACIAS, SL
[Publishing House]
Covadonga, 8
33002 Oviedo - Asturias (Spain)

First edition: February, 2021

ISBN: 978-84-18379-71-0
DL: AS 00257-2021

Dedication.

TO
SIR JOHN P. S. GOBIN,
M. E. Past Grand Master of the Grand Encampment.

To Whom I Am Indebted
For numerous proofs of kindness and sympathy
during the years of our acquaintance,

I dedicate this Monitor.

PREFACE TO FIFTH EDITION.

THE early demand for the Fifth Edition of SHIBBOLETH, a demand the publishers scarcely anticipated in times like these, affords the author an opportunity to add several important matters to the volume, thus rendering it still more valuable to the Order of the Temple. So far as now seen this edition is a complete Monitor.

This edition contains all that appeared in the Fourth Edition, with a few errors corrected, and the Banners of Judah and Persia. There is also added a "Third Appendix," which contains directions for the Reception of Grand Officers; Hints to Eminent Commanders, and Rules of Order; Rituals for Divine Worship; Ritual of a Conclave of Sorrow; Ritual for the Christmas Observance; a Form for Recorder's Minutes; an Arrangement of Asylum and Prelate's Hall; and some Hints on Templar Banquets.

This Monitor reaches farther in its helpfulness than any that has been prepared heretofore. But it has not attempted to describe the Robes, and other equipments not universally accepted by the Order. Many requests have been made for the insertion of such descriptive matter, and the requests have been declined in the interests of peace. Such an attempt would develop acrimonious controversies.

My thanks are due, and they are hereby returned to the Fratres all over the Union, from Maine to Mexico, and the Atlantic to the Pacific, for the kind reception given the former editions of this Monitor, and for the many valuable hints received from all sources. It is the author's sincere desire to make this volume complete in all respects, and he will still be grateful for all suggestions looking to such completeness.

Chattanooga, Tenn., Feb. 10, 1894.

NOTE BY THE PUBLISHERS.

SO far as known, the foregoing Preface is the last word written by SIR GEORGE COOPER CONNOR, the author of this volume. Only a few days later he was forced by disease to the chamber of death, which he never again left until the end came.

The expression of his thanks in the last paragraph may therefore be taken as his loving farewell to his brethren; and it is believed that his earnest desire to provide a Monitor that should be complete and helpful to the members of the Order has been fully realized in this new edition of SHIBBOLETH, to the preparation of which were given the last of his labors on earth.

Nashville, Tenn., November 1, 1894.

THE ILLUSTRIOUS
ORDER OF THE RED CROSS.

Monitorial Instructions, Notes, Comments, and Suggestions.

A FEW HINTS TO COMMANDERS.

IT is the earnest desire of the author of this Monitor to discover that all the Commanderies invest the beautiful, instructive and entertaining Order of the Red Cross with the interest its importance demands. The Ritual provides ample opportunity for the display of true dramatic taste, both in robing and in reading. It also presents the great central thought of the Order,—TRUTH,—as it has never been presented previous to the adoption at Denver.

The feeling had become almost universal that the Order of the Red Cross was of slight importance, and was at best little more than a social observance. Hence the ceremonials were hurried over, the candidate was practically told that it was mere matter of form, and he went away profoundly impressed that the Commandery was indeed a jovial institution. Never was a graver mistake, and the impression so made was more injurious than beneficial. The Ritual now adopted can not fail to correct that erroneous view of the value of the Order.

The Order of the Red Cross should, if possible, be conferred upon classes, and be made the occasion of social intercourse among the members; the healing of wounds, the forming of new bonds of fraternity. The lessons of the ceremonies tend to these noble ends, and by conferring them with the dignity and pathos they merit those ends will be assuredly attained. See with what fervor of gratitude the newly created Companions will hereafter refer to the name they assumed, and the character they represented. There can be no nobler, and if the work is done with the devotion to dramatic effects which the Ritual demands, that name and character will never be forgotten.

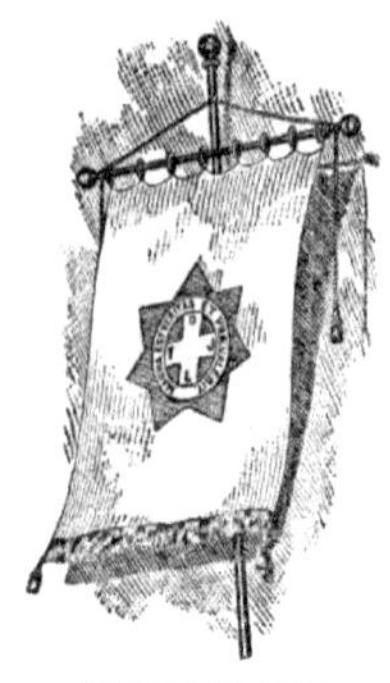

Hence the propriety of the Refection at the close of the work of the Council.

Commanders will advance the interests of the bodies they govern by securing full paraphernalia and equipments. The robes need not be expensive, but should be appropriate. It is of the greatest importance that the Grand Council, Companion Conductor, Warder and Guards be in Jewish robes and turbans. It is equally important that the Persian Guards should wear a uniform different from that of the Order of the Red Cross, an Order not then founded, technically speaking.

The Princes of Persia and the Rulers of Media should wear oriental robes, and the Master of Cavalry should also be in Persian dress. The Sovereign Master, Prince Chancellor and Prince Master of the Palace wear the regulation robes.

The seating of the Princes and Rulers, fully robed, should be in such form as to produce the best effects upon the Jewish Prince. No fixed floor plan can be laid down, because of the variations in the different Audience Chambers. Here Commanders will use their discretion.

In reading the lines of the Addresses be natural above all things. Affect no so-called dramatic or oratorical tones. Invest each scene with earnestness and pathos, as demanded. Allow no frivolous allusions, or undignified liberties to be taken with Z. Play the KING according to your best conception of royalty. See that the Means of Recognition are imparted with great care and accuracy. Let the dignified Order of the Red Cross be indeed a preparation for the solemn Order of the Temple.

THE BANNER OF THE ORDER.

It is of green color. In its center is a star of seven points, painted on gold, within which is painted the blood-red Cross of the Order, surrounded by the Motto: "Magna est Veritas, et Prævalebit." The letters on the arms of the Cross are black.

JEWISH.

PERSIAN.

THE RED CROSS OF THE ORDER.

It is of blood-red color, of equal arms and angles, with the letters on the extremities of the arms, D T J L.

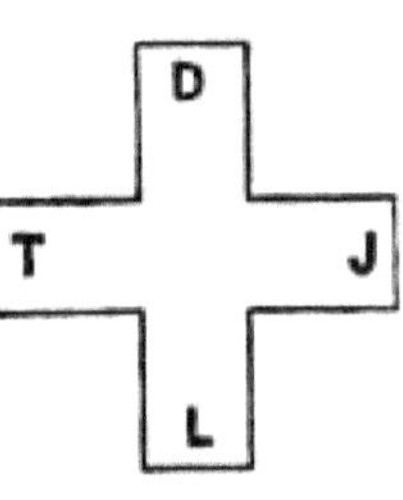

The four arms, thus indicating Deity, Truth, Justice and Liberty, commemorate our faith in God, and in the grand characteristics of the Order.

This Cross is the Jewel of the Order, and may be properly worn by the members thereof, suspended by a green and red ribbon.

ORDER OF THE RED CROSS.

THE learned Sir Alfred Creigh, whose name is a household word among American Knights Templar, used the following language in a report to the Grand Commandery of Pennsylvania, September, 1867:

"The Ritual of the Red Cross was manufactured by Webb and his associates from kindred degrees not of this Order. It requires no argument to demonstrate that this degree has no connection whatever with the orders of Christian knighthood, nor never should have been incorporated into an order whose sublime teachings are of Jesus as the Redeemer of the world—in his mediatorial character, as the way, the truth and the life."

The equally scholarly and thoughtful Sir George S. Blackie made a report to the Grand Commandery of Tennessee, May 9, 1871, in which he used the following strong language:

"The inconsistency is glaring—the ceremonies are foreign to Christian knighthood. How utterly out of place does the Christian candidate appear when, as a preliminary to the glorious truths of the New Testament, he is introduced to a Jewish Sanhedrin, captured by pagan soldiers, and after having been entertained with an apocryphal legend at the banquet of a pagan monarch, he is sent out into the world without having heard of the name of Christ."

The *unanimous* adoption of the revised Ritual of the Illustrious Order of the Red Cross by the Grand Encampment, in Denver, on August 10, 1892, explains and settles the misconceptions of these dear Fratres forever, and yet a few words may not be out of place at this time.

The Illustrious Order of the Red Cross is not a pagan rite, nor is it a mere social observance. It is an Order founded upon TRUTH, recognizing the GOD OF TRUTH as the only one true and living God. As such it is a proper preparation for the solemnities of the Order of the Temple.

Darius believed in the same one that Israel did when he registered a vow with that God to rebuild His Temple in the destroyed city of Jerusalem. No doubt he registered that vow under the promptings of his Jewish friend, Prince Zerubbabel, who was the recognized Chosen of God. Darius kept that vow, demonstrating his love of TRUTH and his reverence for Judah's Jehovah.

The most exalted TRUTH was present implicitly, in Judaism, and the Law of Judaism was the schoolmaster that brought us to Christianity. The most exalted TRUTH is now explicit in Christianity. In Judaism it was the seed, then the blade, and then Christianity ripened it into the ear. So is the TRUTH of all truths implicitly in the Order of the Red Cross, and the candidate finds that same truth, but explicitly, in the Order of the Temple.

As Judaism was a preparation for Christianity, so let, the Illustrious Order of the Red Cross be a preparation for the Christian Order of the Temple.

HISTORICAL SKETCH.

The Scriptures inform us that for their own sins, and those of their forefathers, the Jewish people were led into captivity by Nebuzaradan, chief Captain of Nebuchadnezzar, King of Babylon. As slaves they tilled the valleys of the Euphrates, and of the Tigris, until Cyrus destroyed the Chaldean dynasty.

During that captivity Zerubbabel, Crown Prince of the House of Judah, and Darius, son of Hystaspes, formed an alliance of friendship which was probably terminated with death only.

One of the first acts of the conqueror Cyrus was the liberation of the Jewish captives; he then permitted them to return to Judea, that they might rebuild the city of Jerusalem and its Temple, which Nebuchadnezzar had destroyed.

The foundation stone of the Second Temple was laid 535 years before Christ; Zerubbabel, the Royal Prince, Joshua, the High Priest, and Haggai, the Prophet, laying the same.

Cyrus died, and his son, Cambyses, succeeded him on the Medo-Persian throne. On complaint of the Cutheans, and other contiguous tribes, Cambyses commanded the work upon the city and Temple to cease. During the nine years that followed, scarcely anything was done on the walls of Jerusalem, or its Temple.

Cambyses died and the Magians seized the throne, from which their usurper was driven with great slaughter, in a little over a year. Then the Seven Great Families of Persia laid hold of the government, and Darius ascended the throne. He appointed Zerubbabel, his friend, to be the Governor of the Jews that had returned to Jerusalem under the decree of the great Cyrus, and afterwards made him stand in the royal bed-chamber, as the Guard of his body. There were three of these Guards, and they were chosen because of the monarch's implicit confidence in their loyalty.

Fifteen years after the Jews had laid the foundation of the Second Temple they were forced to call a Grand Council to consult about the state of the country. Cambyses was dead, and the Magian usurper, Smerdis, had been driven from the throne, to give place to Darius, son of Hystaspes, whose favoring of the Jews was believed to be almost as marked as was that of the great Cyrus.

Darius spread a feast at his capital, and invited thereto the Princes of Persia and the Rulers of the Medes. That feast having been thoroughly enjoyed, "they everyone departed to go to bed at their own houses, and Darius, the King, went to bed."

The King slept lightly, and awakening he fell into conversation with his three Guards. He suggested, as a part of the festivities of the morrow, that they three engage in a public discussion of some interesting question, as had been the custom on similar occasions from time immemorial, and that he would reward with a princely gift the successful contestant. The King then proposed the following question:

"Whether Wine was not the strongest? Whether Kings were not such? Whether Women were not such, or whether TRUTH was not strongest of all?"

Esdras makes the Guards suggest both the questions and the prize, but we follow the story as related by Josephus.

Again the King slept, and the Guards prepared for the contest of the morning. When the King arose he sent for the Princes and Rulers to meet him in the Audience Chamber, and witness the contest between his Guards.

This contest began, in time, by one of the Guards declaiming in favor of the strength of Wine, followed by another in favor of the power of the King. Then the Jew, Zerubbabel, contended for the supremacy of Woman, concluding with a noble deliverance in favor of TRUTH.

The brilliant assembly burst forth into applause when Zerubbabel concluded, and the King awarded him the prize in these words: "Ask for somewhat over and above what I have promised, for I would give it unto you because of your wisdom."

Then "Zerubbabel put him in mind of the vow he had made in case he should ever have the kingdom. Now this vow was to build Jerusalem, and to rebuild therein the Temple of God, as also to restore the vessels which Nebuchadnezzar had pillaged and carried to Babylon."

And behold the King was pleased to arise and to kiss his eloquent Guard, and to grant his request. Zerubbabel returned to his people in Jerusalem with great joy, and the rebuilding of the city and Temple was immediately resumed. Darius not only kept his vow, but he made large contributions to the rebuilding out of the royal treasury. The details adapted to more beautifully round out the drama, and to more pointedly teach the lesson of the almighty force and the importance of TRUTH are esoteric.

OFFICERS AND SPECIAL MEMBERS OF A COUNCIL OF THE ILLUSTRIOUS ORDER OF THE RED CROSS:

Sovereign Master	SM	
Prince Chancellor	PC	
Prince Master of the Palace	PMP	
Excellent High Priest	HP	
Master of Cavalry	MC	1
Master of Infantry	MI	2
Master of Finance	MF	3
Master of Dispatches	MD	4
Standard Bearer	StB	5
Sword Bearer	SwB	6
Warder	W	7
Sentinel	Sen.	
Guards	Gd	0
Princes and Rulers	○	

The Sovereign Master, Prince Chancellor and Prince Master of the Palace will wear the regulation oriental robes. The Master of Cavalry should be in Persian Uniform, and not in the Uniform of the Red Cross. The members designated as the Princes and Rulers should be in oriental dress. The Uniform of the Red Cross is as follows:

Green Sash, Belt and Sword. A Red Cross may be on the Sash. A Cap, with the Red Cross of the Order in front.

A Companion of the Red Cross should always appear in the Audience Chamber clad in dark garments.

The "Fatigue Uniform" of a Knight Templar should not appear in the ceremonies of the Order of the Red Cross. The Templar Baldric turned inside out will serve as a Sash. If the Passion Cross on the Templar Cap is movable it can be replaced by the Red Cross of the Order, or a cover, on which is the Red Cross of the Order, may be put on the Templar Cap. The Templar Sword will be sufficient.

In the Grand Council the High Priest wears the regulation Robes of the Royal Arch Chapter, but these should not be worn by him in the Audience Chamber.

The Grand Council should be clothed in Jewish Robes and Turbans, as should also be the Companion Conductor and Warder, while in attendance upon the Grand Council. The Jewish Guards should also be in Jewish Robes and Turbans.

When a Commandery is unable to furnish these Jewish Robes, the members of the Grand Council, Companion Conductor, Guards and Warder should appear in plain civilian dress, and *not* in Red Cross Uniform, while in attendance upon the Grand Council.

It is of importance that full equipments should be provided for the ceremonies of the Red Cross. These equipments should be prepared with good taste, and should always be kept in good order and ready for immediate use.

The Fetters, Garb of Slavery, Robe and Coronet should be easily put on and taken off.

The "Altar of Masonry" may be small, so as to be easily moved from place to place, and may be placed in the northwest corner of the Audience Chamber, ready for use when called for.

The "Bridge" and the "Banners" in the discretion of the Commanderies.

TO OPEN A COUNCIL
OF THE RED CROSS.

THE Council Chamber is suitably arrayed under the direction of the Prince Master of the Palace.

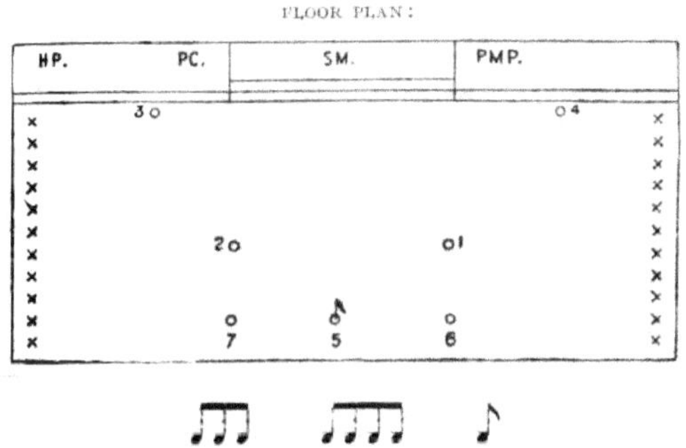

RECEPTION OF SOVEREIGN MASTER.

* * * *
* *

PRAYER.

ALMIGHTY and Eternal Jehovah, the only living and true God whose throne is in the heavens, yet who regardest alike the princes and the people that dwell upon earth, we desire to thank thee for the many mercies and blessings with which thou hast been pleased to crown our lives. We thank thee for this social and fraternal intercourse with our Companions. Be mercifully near us at all times, and give us the aid of thy Holy Spirit to guide us into all TRUTH. Grant us thy grace to cheer and strengthen us in our journey through life, and deliverance from the snares and pitfalls of the Evil One. Incline our hearts to seek thy favor and protection, as our rightful Sovereign, that we may not be impeded in the great work of erecting a spiritual edifice that shall endure forever. Pardon all our sins, we beseech thee, and finally admit us into the presence of the King of Kings, as members of his eternal household. AMEN! Response, AMEN!

OR THIS:

MERCIFUL Father, have mercy upon us, we beseech thee; put understanding in our minds, enlighten our eyes, and cause our hearts to cleave to thy law. Because we have trusted in thy Name we will rejoice and be glad in thy salvation, and in thy mercies, O Lord, our God. Cause us to cleave unto thy great Name forever, and bring upon us from the four corners of the earth the blessing of peace, harmony and prosperity. Blessed art thou, O Lord God, who hast chosen thy people in love. And when we have accomplished thy will upon earth receive us to thyself, and unto thy great and holy Name shall be the glory for ever and ever. AMEN! Response, AMEN.

* * * *
 * *

SIGNS.

* * * *
 * *

REHEARSAL OF DUTIES.

In this rehearsal each Officer, when addressed, will arise and SALUTE. * * * The Officer will come to Carry Swords, and stand firm until the close of the Ceremonial, or until a subsequent order issued to him * * *

THE WORK.

The Council of the Illustrious Order of the Red Cross being open, and the COUNCIL HALL being properly equipped for the formation of the Grand Council.

* * * *
 * *

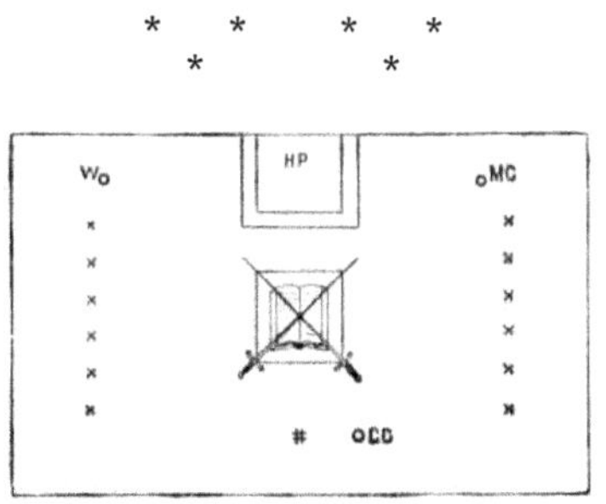

HIGH PRIEST'S ADDRESS.

* * * *
 * *

THE RECORDS OF OUR FATHERS.

Now in the second year of their coming unto the house of God at Jerusalem, in the second month, began Zerubbabel the son of Shealtiel, and Jeshua the son of Jozadak, and the remnant of their brethren the priests and the Levites and all they that were come out of the captivity unto Jerusalem; and appointed the Levites, from twenty years old and upward, to set forward the work of the house of the Lord. Then stood Jeshua *with* his sons and his brethren, Cadmiel and his sons, the sons of Judah, together, to set forward the workmen in the house of God: the sons of Henadad, *with* their sons and their brethren the Levites. And when the builders laid the foundation of the temple of the Lord, they set the priests in their apparel with trumpets, and the Levites the sons of Asaph with cymbals, to praise the Lord, after the ordinance of David king of Israel. And they sang together by course in praising and giving thanks unto the Lord; because *he is* good, for his mercy *endureth* forever toward Israel. And all the people shouted with a great shout, when they praised the Lord, because the foundation of the house of the Lord was laid.

Now when the adversaries of Judah and Benjamin heard that the children of the captivity builded the temple unto the Lord

God of Israel; then they came to Zerubbabel, and to the chief of the fathers, and said unto them, Let us build with you: for we seek your God, as ye *do;* and we do sacrifice unto him since the days of Esarhaddon king of Assur, which brought us up hither. But Zerubbabel, and Jeshua, and the rest of the chief of the fathers of Israel, said unto them, Ye have nothing to do with us to build an house unto our God; but we ourselves together will build unto the Lord God of Israel, as king Cyrus the king of Persia hath commanded us. Then the people of the land weakened the hands of the people of Judah, and troubled them in building, and hired counsellors against them, to frustrate their purpose, all the days of Cyrus king of Persia, even until the reign of Darius king of Persia. And in the reign of Ahasuerus, in the beginning of his reign, wrote they *unto him* an accusation against the inhabitants of Judah and Jerusalem. And in the days of Artaxerxes wrote Bishlam, Mithredath, Tabeel, and the rest of their companions, unto Artaxerxes king of Persia; and the writing of the letter *was* written in the Syrian tongue, and interpreted in the Syrian tongue. Rehum the chancellor and Shimshai the scribe wrote a letter against Jerusalem to Artaxerxes the king in this sort: This *is* the copy of the letter that they sent unto him, *even* unto Artaxerxes the king; Thy servants the men on this side of the river, and at such a time. Be it known unto the king, that the Jews which came up from thee to us are come unto Jerusalem, building the rebellious and the bad city, and have set up the walls *thereof,* and joined the foundations. Be it known now unto the king, that, if this city be builded, and the walls set up *again,* *then* will they not pay toll, tribute, and custom, and *so* thou shalt endamage the revenue of the kings. Now because we have maintenance from *the king's* palace, and it was not meet for us to see the king's dishonor, therefore have we sent and certified the king; that search may be made in the book of the records of thy fathers: so shalt thou find in the book of the records, and know that this city *is* a rebellious city, and hurtful unto kings and provinces, and that they have moved sedition within the same of old time: for which cause was this city destroyed. We certify the king that, if this city be builded *again,* and the walls thereof set up, by this means thou shalt have no portion on this side the river. *Then* sent the king an answer unto Rehum the chancellor, and to Shimshai the scribe, and *to* the rest of their companions that dwell in Samaria, and *unto* the rest beyond the river, Peace, and at such a time. The letter which ye sent unto us hath been plainly read before me. And I commanded, and search hath been made, and it is found that this city of old time hath made insurrection against kings, and *that* rebellion and sedition have been made therein. There have been mighty kings also over Jerusalem, which have ruled over all *countries* beyond the river; and toll, tribute, and custom, was paid unto them. Give ye now commandment to cause these men to cease, and that this city be not builded, until *another* commandment shall be given from me. Take heed now that ye fail not to do this: why should damage grow to the hurt of the kings? Now when the copy of king Arta-xerxes' letter *was* read before Rehum, and Shimshai the scribe, and their companions, they went up in haste to Jerusalem unto the Jews, and made them to cease by force and power. Then ceased the work of the house of God which *is* at Jerusalem. So it ceased unto the second year of the reign of Darius king of Persia.

* *   *   *
*   *

PLEDGES OF FIDELITY.

* *   *   *
*   *

THE SWORD.

The glittering blade of the Sword entrusted to a Representative of the Grand Council should symbolize tie purity of his intentions.

* *   *   *
*   *

THE GREEN SASH.

* *   *   *
*   *

The color of his Sash should in all places bring him cheering and hallowed memories.

* *   *   *
*   *

THE JOURNEY.

The road from Jerusalem to Susa, the chief treasury of Persia, and one of the favorite cities of the Persian kings, lay in part through the country restored to the Jews by the decree of Cyrus, but after crossing the Euphrates it was entirely in the domain of King Darius. Indeed, a more cautious statement would limit the Jewish country to west of the Jordan.

The Jews attempted, in an embarrassed way, to picket their own country, and to provide passes with which to distinguish their friends. The domain of the Persian monarch was under strict military surveillance, and countersigns were absolutely necessary to travel therein with safety.

Darius lived in daily dread of spies and secret enemies front among the defeated, though not destroyed, Magians. The discipline of the empire was sternly strict, and the slightest suspicion of disloyalty led to captivity and death.

*   *   *   *
*   *

IN THE PRESENCE OF THE KING.

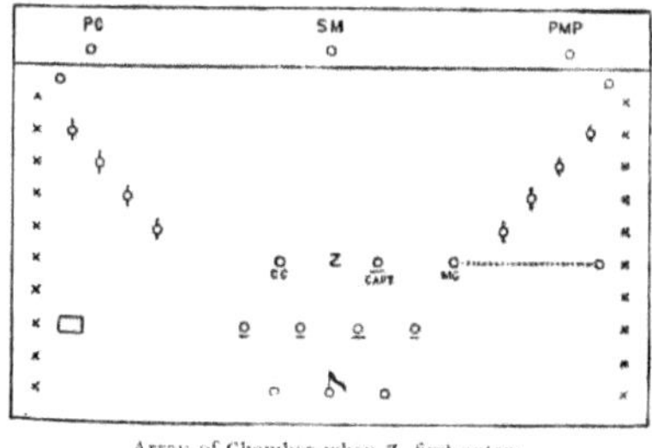

Array of Chamber when Z. first enters.

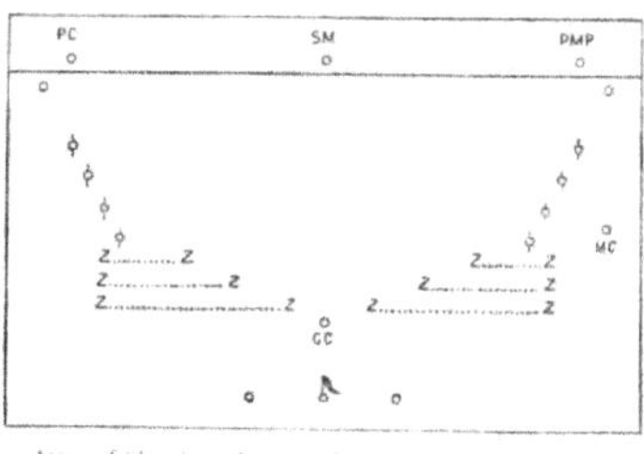

Array of Chamber when CC. rises to speak for all the Z's. Princes of Persia, and Rulers of Medes who are in robes and Coronets.

THE IMMEMORIAL DISCUSSION.

On the morning succeeding the great feast at the capital of the Persian empire, Darius listened to the oratorical contests of the three Guards of the Bed-chamber, in reply to the question, "Which is the greatest, the strength of WINE, the power of the KING, or the influence of WOMAN?"

THE STRENGTH OF WINE.

O ye Princes and Rulers, how exceeding strong is Wine! it causeth all men to err that drink it; it maketh the mind of the King and the beggar to be all one; of the bondman and freeman, of the poor man and the rich; it turneth also every thought into jollity and mirth, so that a man remembereth neither sorrow nor debt; it changeth and elevateth the spirits, and enliveneth the heavy hearts of the miserable. It maketh a man forget his brethren and draw his sword against his best friends. O ye Princes and Rulers, is not Wine the strongest, that forceth us to do these things?

THE POWER OF THE KING.

It is beyond dispute, O Princes and Rulers, that God has made man master of all things under the sun; to command them, to make use of them, and to apply them to his service as he pleases; but, whereas men have only dominion over other sublunary creatures, Kings have an authority even over men themselves, and a right of ruling them by will and pleasure.

Now, he that is master of those who are masters of all things else, hath no earthly thing above him.

* * * *
* *

THE INFLUENCE OF WOMAN.

O Princes and Rulers, the force of wine is not to be denied, neither is that of Kings, that unites so many men in one common bond of allegiance; but, the supereminency of Woman is yet above all this: for Kings are but the gifts of women, and they are also the mothers of those that cultivate our vineyards.

Women have power to make us abandon our very country and relations, and many times to forget the best friends we have in the world, and, forsaking all other comforts, to live and die with them.

But when all is said, neither they, nor Wine, nor Kings are comparable to the almighty force of Truth.

As for all other things, they are mortal and transient, but Truth alone is unchangeable and everlasting; the benefits we receive from it are subject to no variations or vicissitudes of time or fortune.

In her judgment is no unrighteousness, and she is the strength, wisdom, power, and majesty of all ages.

* * * *
* *

"Great is TRUTH, and mighty above all things."

"BLESSED BE THE GOD OF TRUTH."

THE PLEA FOR REMEMBRANCE.

O King, remember thy vow, which thou hast vowed, to build Jerusalem in the day when thou shouldst come to thy kingdom, and restore the holy vessels which were taken away out of Jerusalem. Thou hast also vowed to build up the Temple, which was burned when Judah was made desolate by the Chaldees.

And now, O King, this is that I desire of thee, that thou make good the vow, the performance whereof with thine own mouth thou hast vowed to the King of Heaven.

*   *   *   *
*   *

THE DECREE.

Moreover, I make a decree what ye shall do to the elders of these Jews for the building of this house of God: that of the king's goods, *even* of the tribute beyond the river, forthwith expenses be given unto these men, that they be not hindered. And that which they have need of, both young bullocks, and rams, and lambs, for the burnt offerings of the God of heaven, wheat, salt, wine, and oil, according to the appointment of the priests which *are* at Jerusalem, let it be given them day by day without fail: that they may offer sacrifices of sweet savours unto the God of heaven, and pray for the life of the king, and of his sons. Also I have made a decree, that whosoever shall alter this word, let timber be pulled down from his house, and being set up, let him be hanged thereon; and let his house be made a dunghill for this. Ezra vi: 8-11.

FOUNDING THE NEW ORDER.

* * * *
* *

THE VOW.

1. 2. 3. 4. 5. 6.

The Princes of Persia and Rulers of the Medes having arisen to witness the Vow, resume their seats with approbation.

* * * *
* *

THE GREEN SASH.

To the Royal Prince it was a perpetual incentive to the performance of every duty; to a Companion of the Red Cross it is a reminder that TRUTH is a divine attribute, and the foundation of every virtue.

* * * *
* *

THE SWORD.

It is worthy of being worn by a Companion of the Red Cross, as well as by the Crown Prince of the House of Judah.

* * * *
* *

MEANS OF RECOGNITION.

* * * *
* *

THE BANNER OF THE ORDER.

The Banner of the Order is of green color. In its center there is a Star of seven points, within which is a red Cross of equal arms and angles, surrounded by the MOTTO: "*Magna est Veritas, et Prævalebit,*"– "Great is Truth, and it will Prevail."

THE CROSS OF THE ORDER.

The Cross of the Order is of equal arms and angles, of blood-red color, with the letters D T J L on the extremities of the arms. The arms indicate DEITY, TRUTH, JUSTICE, LIBERTY.

* * * *
* *

THE WELCOME.

With joy the new Companion is welcomed to a seat among his Companions.

* * * *
* *

THE BANQUET.

Never was banquet spread under more joyous surroundings. It is invariably served after the Council closes, if served at all.

TO CLOSE THE COUNCIL.

The same precautionary steps precede the Closing as precede the Opening of a Council of the Illustrious Order of the Red Cross.

The   Sovereign   Master, in his discretion, may hold Rehearsal of Duties before closing.

*   *   *   *
  *   *

PRAYER

O LORD our God, we thank thee, we praise thee, we magnify thee for the gift of thy holy Light. Make it to shine into our hearts, and write thy Law upon our consciences.

And now as we go out into, the world again may the words of our mouths, and the meditations of our hearts, be acceptable in thy sight, O Lord, our strength and our redeemer. AMEN! Response, AMEN!

*   *   *   *
  *   *

S.M.–Companions, the priceless Jewels of humanity are "the beauty of LOVE, the charm of FRIENDSHIP, the sacredness of SORROW, the heroism of PATIENCE, the courage of TRUTH"! Go in peace, and, "May the Lord bless thee, and keep thee: the Lord make his face shine upon thee, and be gracious unto thee: the Lord lift up his countenance upon thee, and give thee peace."

THREE ANCIENT CITIES OF PERSIA.

PERSEPOLIS.—This was the chief city, or capital, of the Persian kingdom proper. Alexander destroyed it, and Darius Hystaspes is supposed to have founded it. To-day its ruins stand in the valley of Schiraz, the wonder of the world. These ruins are an immense platform, fifty feet above the plain, hewn partly out of the mountain itself, the remainder built of marble blocks from twenty to sixty feet in length, so nicely fitted together that the joints are scarcely discernible to-day. This platform is fourteen hundred feet long, and nine hundred feet wide, and faces the four quarters of the world. The ascent from the plain is made by marble steps, passing colossal figures, until you reach the gigantic columns, with their beautiful capitals, twelve to fifteen feet in circumference, and fifty feet high, which supported the cedar roof that protected the residents from the hot sun. And there you see rows of carved images, men of every nation and clime.

This was the palace of Darius. To this palace Ahasuerus may have brought his fair Jewish wife, Esther, from Tusa, and from there had her conducted to the other palace still farther up the mountain, which the drunken Alexander burned B. C. 330.

SUSA, or SHUSHAN.—So named because of the lilies that abounded in the valley. In Daniel's time it was in possession of the Babylonians, but when Cyrus conquered Babylon he transferred it to Persia.

It was from this city of Shushan that Darius issued his decree for the rebuilding of Jerusalem, and its Temple, it being the winter residence of Darius, and of all the Persian kings after Cyrus. In gratitude for this decree the Jews called the eastern gate of the Second Temple the Gate of Shushan. It is said that a resemblance of the city of Shushan was engraved upon that gate.

ECBATANA.—This was a city of the Medes, a beautiful place, and after the union of the Medes and Persians became a favorite summer residence of the Persian monarchs.

In this city is shown to-day the tombs of Mordecai and Esther, but why they should have been interred in that city is a mystery.

It was in Ecbatana that Cyrus held his capital, and in its archives, therefore, was found the roll which proved to Darius that Cyrus had made a decree allowing the Jews to rebuild the Temple.

It is held by many that it was in this city of Ecbatana that Zoroaster made his first appearance.

THE RELIGION OF THE ANCIENT PERSIANS.

Up to the seizure of the throne by Smerdis the Magian religion was dominant among the Medes and Persians. That religion abominated the worship of images, as Judaism did, and worshiped the One God only by fire. This religion fell into disgrace when its chief, Smerdis, was driven from the throne with such awful slaughter. Darius was a Magian at that time, and for some time afterwards.

Sabianism was idolatry, the opposite of Magianism, but it gained favor on the disgrace of the Magians. This religion consisted chiefly in the worship of the host of heaven,—hence the name from *tsaba*, host,—and the worship of the planets. In his later life this religion became so powerful that Darius gave it his adherence.

CONCLUDING REMARKS.

Acti labores jucundi

THE captives released under the decree of the great Cyrus, issued B. C. 536, entered the desolated city of Jerusalem on the 10th day of Tebeth, B. C. 535, under the leadership of Zerubbabel. On the 23d day of Adar, B. C. 515, the Second Temple was completed. It was dedicated, and the Priests and Levites assigned to their duties.

The second installment of returning captives entered Jerusalem on the 10th of Schebet, B. C. 458, under the leadership of Ezra. He began a reformation of the people by compelling them to put away their unbelieving wives. The poor, impoverished, rain-soaked people obeyed the imperative commands of this lineal descendant of Aaron when they had assembled themselves in the city, five months afterwards. They put away the wives they had brought up with them from Babylon, kept a solemn fast, and entered into a covenant to walk in God's law, as given them by his servant Moses.

The third installment entered Jerusalem, under the guidance of Nehemiah, B. C. 445, when Nehemiah became Governor.

Those who, for various reasons, preferred to remain in the Persian country, were henceforth known as "The Dispersion."

On the first day of Nisan, B. C. 445, a solemn fast was held, by order of Nehemiah, and on the 24th day of the same month there was another. At these Ezra read the Book of the Law of Moses to the people, and after seven days they "rejoiced and feasted as they had not done since the days of Joshua, the son of Nun." It was then they covenanted to keep the seventh day, and the seventh year.

Thus was Israel re-established in Jerusalem, and the city and its Temple rebuilt. Other cities were built, and peace was within their walls, and prosperity within their palaces.

The ceremonials of the Illustrious Order of the Red Cross furnish ample scope for the best of elocutionary work. Dignity of manner, clearness of enunciation, and careful reading of the lines are absolutely necessary to the full development of the Ritual.

A true Mason will lay down his life rather than surrender his integrity. A Companion of the Red Cross holds his engagements sacred and inviolable, and will not accept favors or emoluments at the sacrifice of his integrity. Nor will he draw his sword in the cause of Injustice, Falsehood, or Oppression, for JUSTICE, TRUTH, and LIBERTY are the Grand Characteristics of that Illustrious Order.

Endurance, coupled with faith and perseverance, is a shining characteristic of a Companion of the Red Cross. He is taught a lesson he never forgets in the secession of the Ten Tribes of Israel, when told by Rehoboam, the son of Solomon, that his father chastised them with whips, but that he would chastise them with scorpions. They withdrew from their allegiance, and left the tribes of JUDAH and BENJAMIN in possession of Jerusalem, its Temple, and the traditions. Their lack of patience and endurance, under such trying circumstances, resulted in their disappearance as tribes, or as a people. And to-day the Jews, scattered all over the face of the earth, claim descent from the two patient tribes,—Judah and Benjamin.

Those who seek to destroy their neighbors often overreach themselves as did that Governor and nobleman of the Medo-Persian domain,—TATNAI and SHETHAR-BOZNAI. The search among the archives, in Ecbatana, which they petitioned Darius to have made, resulted in the discovery of the Decree made by Cyrus, which overthrew their hopes of preventing the rebuilding of Jerusalem and its Temple. God often causes the wrath of man to praise him.

There is carved upon the Corner-Stone of the Illustrious Order of the Red Cross this Motto: "VERITAS *prævalebit.*" And surely an Order so grounded is of infinite importance to the human family. Verily, TRUTH will prevail.

A Companion of the Red Cross has engraved upon his escutcheon these words: "LIBERTAS *et natale solum*." Can such a man be other than a good citizen? Aye, such men are willing to shed their blood in defense of liberty and native land.

"Wo unto them that decree unrighteous decrees, and that write the injustice that they have adjudged. Judge the poor with righteousness, and according to equity relieve the lowly ones of earth. Execute true judgment, and cause every one to show mercy and compassion to his brother; and let none oppress the widow nor the fatherless, the stranger nor the poor."

The origin of the device of the EAGLE on royal banners can be traced to very early periods. It was the ensign of the ancient Kings of the Medo-Persian empire, of Persia and Babylon. The device was adopted by Charlemagne to denote the union of the black eagle of the east with the golden eagle of the west, typifying the "Holy Roman Empire."

Sceptre (*Greek*, skeptron; Hebrew, *shebet*) means rod of command, or staff of authority. It is the sign of power and authority, and is therefore to be preferred, in the Creation of a Companion, to the use of a Sword.

This was the promise: Zerubbabel was appointed Governor, or Tirshatha (Ezra ii: 63), of Judah by Darius. Of Zerubbabel God said: "Speak now to Zerubbabel the son of Shealtiel, governor of Judah, and to Joshua the son of Josedech, the high priest, and to the residue of the people, saying, Who *is* left among you that saw this house in her first glory? and how do ye see it now? is *it* not in your eyes in comparison of it as nothing? " Haggai ii: 2, 3.

"The hands of Zerubbabel have laid the foundation of this house; his hands shall also finish it." Zechariah iv: 9.

SWORD CUTS–PASSES.

It is important to the purposes of this Monitor to describe only three Cuts, and the Thrust. These are Ritualistic, and not military. The regular Cuts of the Sword are: On left shoulder, ONE; on right shoulder, TWO; on left leg, THREE; on right leg, FOUR. This is the succession, ritualistically speaking: Two, ONE, THREE, FOUR.

The following illustrates these Cuts. The Swords numbered "1" are of the First Division, and those numbered "2" are of the Second Division. The Cuts are counted in illustration as given, and not as regularly numbered Sword Cuts.

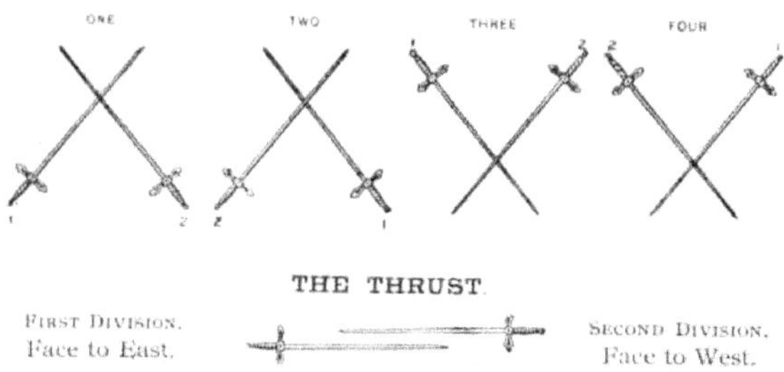

These Cuts should be executed with the flat of the blade, and not with the edge. The same side of the blade touches in every Cut. It is important to remember this, and thereby avoid the awkward efforts sometimes made to reverse the blade at each Cut.

These Cuts also illustrate "Over an Arch of Steel" (Cut Three) and "Under an Arch of Steel" (Cut One).

"SALUTE" AND "PRESENT."

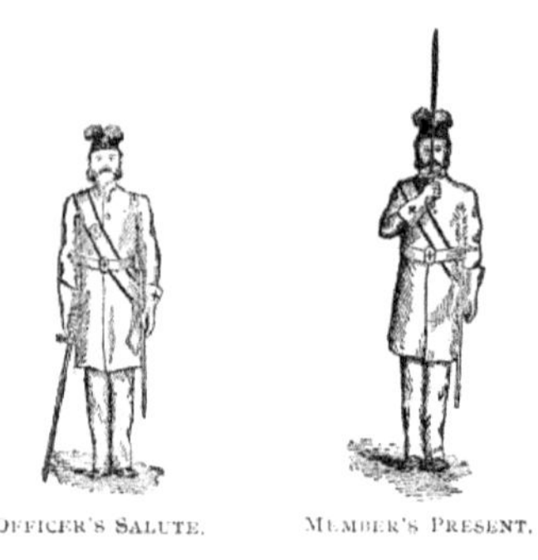

OFFICER'S SALUTE.   MEMBER'S PRESENT.

ORDER OF THE TEMPLE.

Monitorial Instructions, Notes, Comments, and Suggestions.

HISTORY OF THE ORDER OF THE TEMPLE.

IN the year of our Lord 1118 the following gentlemen formed themselves into a society, in the city of Jerusalem, whose duty it was to escort pilgrims to and from the Holy City, through the mountain defiles and dangerous passes, en route, viz.: Hugh de Payen, a gentleman named Rossal, Godfrey de St. Omer, Godfrey Bissol, Payen de Montdidier, Archambaud de Saint-Aignan, and two gentlemen named D'Andre and De Gondemare, respectively. These eight were joined by Hugh of Champagne seven years later. And the society thus formed was without rules, and its members wore no particular habit.

They lived in a house close by the Temple, and soon came to be known as Knights of the Temple, and Templars. That house was a part of the palace of the western kings, which had been set apart as the home of the pilgrims, and their guards. The Church of the Holy Sepulchre was the chapel of the new society.

Hugh de Payen went to Rome in 1127 to ask of Pope Honorius II a new crusade, and while there besought his Holiness to form the little society at Jerusalem into a religious and military order. The Pope referred him to the Council of Troyes, then in session, which appointed St. Bernard to draw up rules for the Order, and prescribe for it a dress. The white dress prescribed by St. Bernard had a red cross added by Pope Eugenius III, years afterwards.

The name assumed by this society is not known to us with perfect accuracy. They were known as "The Brethren of the Order of the Temple," and as "Brethren of the Soldiery of the Temple," and as "Brethren of the Temple." They were referred to as "*Pauperes Commilitones Christi et Templi Solomonis.*" It is supposed that their armorial bearing of two knights riding one horse referred to this poverty, but that is not certain. Neither is it clear that the bearing alluded to "Brotherly Love," or even to "Humility." True they were vowed to chastity, poverty, and obedience, but the king supplied all their wants in the beginning, and the Order soon began to revel in opulence.

The enthusiasm which this society of *nine* gallant young gentlemen aroused all over Christendom tells the story of the popular craze. The Pope, Prelates, Kings, and all the people, praised their chivalry, and eager youths clamored for admission to their ranks. The Pope promised heaven to all who would take the Cross against the Saracens. Kings settled rich estates upon the new Order, on which Priories were founded. The Order increased in numbers with astounding rapidity. They were young nobles of hot blood, of sinews of steel, and of great physical endurance. These became Templars knowing that they were to be forever upon the field, and never to know peace.

The Templars had no lady-love save Mary, Queen of Heaven; they wore no ornaments, their hair was to be kept short, and their dress plain white. They were to eat two and two at the same table, so that each might know that the other did not fast, which was strictly forbidden. They were to attend chapel services, but if on duty at that time they might say their prayers in bed. They were to hold no correspondence with the outer world, nor could a Brother walk alone. Amusements were not encouraged, and all conversation was serious. The Templar had no personal wealth, and if he was taken prisoner by the Saracen he was to be left to his fate,—no ransom could be paid for him. The Templar well knew that his fate was the alternative of the Koran or the sword. Hugh de Payen took three hundred such men back to Jerusalem with him, and before five years had passed every one of these had been killed.

The Hospitalers, which had been organized into a military order by Godfrey de Bouillon, became envious of the reputation of the Templars, and dissensions arose, though both frequently fought gallantly side by side against the common enemy. The dissensions began as early as 1179, and continued, with frequent reconciliations, until the suppression of the Order of the Temple, in 1314. In 1251 the two Orders actually fought a battle, in which the Templars were almost cut to pieces. But their decimated ranks were speedily filled.

We need not attempt to give even a summary of the great battles that were fought by the Templars, or recite even instances of their almost superhuman prowess. Time and space would fail us. Princes came to fear them, and bishops to hate them. What cared they? They were rich; there were no scandals afloat; they were both churchmen and warriors; their nation was the Catholic Church; their only chief the Pope. They mixed in no struggles unless the Pope's interests were involved; their persons were sacred. They ever held up the Cross against the Crescent. They were proportionally hated, and their counsels were rejected when they could have secured by treaty free access to Jerusalem, and peace with the Soldans in the last crusade. Poor William of Sonnac! His eye had just been dashed out, and he hastened to plead with the Christian chiefs to enter into treaty. His advice was scorned. Then dashing the blood from his eyeless socket he rushed to horse, and wildly shouted, "Beauceant to the front! Beauceant and death!" He and all his companions fell sword in hand that day. Aye, there never was known a Templar who was a coward.

In 1301 Boniface III was Pope, and Philip the Fair was King of France. A feud broke out between them, Boniface claiming temporal power in France. The Templars, as usual, stood by the Pope, and they sent him funds. Boniface died within two years, and his successor, Benedict XI, died within the year of his exaltation. This was the opportunity for Philip, who by intriguing and promises secured the election of the ambitious Archbishop of Bordeaux. He assumed the tiara under the title of Clement V. He had agreed to live in France, and was to do the bidding of Philip. Clement approved the demand which Philip had made upon the priests for subsidies, and said nothing about the Templars being compelled to likewise submit to these taxations. In fact, Philip had called Boniface "His *Fatuity*" in place of "His Holiness," and burned the Pope's Bull of Excommunication with great eclat. Then he made a prisoner of the Holy Father, which created a great scandal.

Clement V was wiser than Boniface III, and Philip had in him an unswerving ally when he sought to suppress the Templars, who sided with his enemy, Boniface III, and desired to gather into the treasury of France the immense riches of that Order. The Templars never suspected for a moment that their only master, the Pope, would betray them; and, in fact, had not a suspicion of their danger. They lived so haughtily apart from all the world that no hint of the King's desire to procure testimony against them reached their ears. But it reached the ears of others, among whom were two renegades, one a Knight Templar disgraced from the dignity of Prior, the other a member of the Order dismissed for infamous impieties. These wretches were Esquin von Florian, Prior of Montfaucon, the other one Noffodei. They were in prison at Paris, and under sentence of death.

These villains informed their jailer that if their lives were spared they would put the King in possession of the secret impieties of the Templars. The King examined them himself; and the revelations they made, among others, were:

1. The Templars were more like Mohammedans than Christians.

2. The Novices were required to deny Christ, and to spit upon the Cross.

3. The Templars worshiped idols, despised the sacraments, murdered, and secretly buried all betrayers of their secrets, and practiced theft and sodomy.

4. The Templars betrayed the Holy Land to the Infidels.

Philip took down these accusations, and pretended to believe them, although he knew that no intimation of such crimes had even been whispered in any of the states of Christendom, in which the Templars lived and held rich preceptories.

We may well spare the reader a recital of the deceptions, mis-representations, hypocrisy and falsehoods that attended the so-called inquiries made into those charges by the Pope and his bishops. De Molai had been to see the Pope, in response to an affectionate letter from His Holiness, although the charges were in his hands over a year before writing so affectionately. The Pope did not allude to the accusations, and De Molai had not heard of them. The Grand Master came with a band of trusted Knights, and twelve mules laden with chests of gold and silver. The wily Philip received him without signs of displeasure. It was now 1306, nearly two years since the accusations had been made. Rumors at last reached the Grand Master, and he grew uneasy. He went again to the Pope (1307) taking with him the four French preceptors, and earnestly denied the stories that he had heard. The Pope dismissed him as if he believed the Order inno-cent.

The conduct of both the Pope and the King lulled the Tem-plars to absolute security all over France, and they continued to live on in haughty and friendless isolation until the morning of October 13, 1307, when every Templar in France was seized in his bed and carried to prison. The King gave the secret order of arrest, and the bishops, whom the Templars had so long defied, cordially co-operated, and flung them into their filthy dungeons.

Let us omit the farce of a trial, and relate some incidents. The prisoners died rapidly of hunger and exposure while being plied with promises of liberty if they would confess the guilt of the Grand Master, and of the Order. They were assured that the Grand Master had already confessed. A few said "yes," but the mass denied the infamous accusations. Many cried out,—"If the Grand Master so confessed he lied in his throat." These were brutally tortured, and thirty-six of them perished in the tortures. Some broke down and confessed, but withdrew the confession when the tortures had ceased. The poor Pope in horror protested, but the King accused him of trying to conceal the guilt of the Order. The inquiry went on, traitors confessed, Templars were deceived, and came to Paris under lying promises.

It is probable that under torture De Molai, an old man, emaciated by brutal treatment in prison, confessed to the guilt of the Order. But before the Church Commission he appeared stupefied when he heard the confession read. He cried out that the confession was false, averring that he could stand boiling, roasting, or even killing, but that prolonged tortures were beyond human endurance. His hands had been crushed until the blood ran from his nails. Others had had their feet held to the fire until they had dropped off. Confessions were made, and almost immediately withdrawn. A squabble arose between the Papal Commission and the Court of the Archbishop of Sens. This latter court assumed jurisdiction, and burned fifty-four of the Templars in one batch, on the spot where afterwards stood the infamous Bastile. The Commission mildly objected, and finally agreed upon a report that the Order of the Temple had disgraced itself; and should be suppressed. Pope Clement V approved the recommendation, and the Order was officially suppressed.

The tragic end of Grand Master De Molai is worthy of permanent record. The Bull of Suppression was read on a platform set up in the Cathedral Church, on March 18, 1314, and in the presence of the Grand Master and the Priors of France and Aquitaine. When the Cardinal read the vile charges De Molai cried with a loud voice that they were false, but the two Priors, terrified by death at the stake, adhered to their confessions. On the edge of the platform De Molai spoke: "I declare before heaven and earth, and I avow, although to my eternal shame, that I have committed the greatest of all crimes; but only by acknowledging the truth of those so foully charged against an Order, of which the truth to-day compels me to say that Order is innocent. The fearful spectacle that fronts me can not make me confirm a first lie by a second. Upon a condition so infamous, I heartily renounce a life already hateful to me."

As the sun went down that same evening the Grand Master perished in the flames on the island in the Seine, professing the innocence of the Order, and welcoming to the same fate one of the Priors who feared to stand by him in the cathedral, but who rallied, and died beside him. It is said that the dying Grand Master summoned both King and Pope to meet him at the judgment. Clement died within a few weeks, in great physical agony, and a vicious horse sent the cruel Philip to his account within a year thereafter.

So ended the ancient Order of the Templars. They were needed no longer, since Palestine had been abandoned to the Infidel. "Empires, monarchies, guilds, orders, societies, religious creeds, rise in the same way, and disappear when they stand in the way of other things."

HISTORY OF THE ORDER IN THE UNITED STATES.

"It would be a matter of pride and gratification," said Past Grand Master Hopkins, in his report to Grand Encampment, in 1889, "if we could trace the genealogy of our Templar organizations, by clear and unquestionable steps, back to a legitimate and respected parentage. But as that can not be done—as the very baptismal record of our Grand Encampment has been found to be erroneous—and so many subordinate bodies were formed without formality and without legality, we can only admit the established facts, and trust that the power, the purity, and the renown of our maturer years may soften the disappointment occasioned by the knowledge of an unfortunate origin."

The Grand Encampment was formed on the 10th of June, 1816, by delegates from the Grand Commanderies (then called Encampments) of Massachusetts, Rhode Island and New York.

CONCLAVES AND GRAND MASTERS OF THE GRAND ENCAMPMENT

NO.	CONCLAVES.		GRAND MASTERS.	REMARKS.
	Place.	*Year.*	*Name and Residence.*	
1	New York	1816	DeWitt Clinton, New York	
2	New York	1819	DeWitt Clinton, New York	
3	New York	1826	DeWitt Clinton, New York	Died February 11, 1828.
4	New York	1829	Rev. Jonathan Nye, Claremont	Died April 1, 1843.
5	Baltimore	1832	Rev. Jonathan Nye, Claremont	
6	Washington	1835	James M. Allen, Cayuga, N. Y	Died
7	Boston	1838	James M. Allen, Cayuga, N. Y	
8	New York	1841	James M Allen Cayuga, N. Y	
9	New Haven	1844	Archibald Bull, Troy, N. Y	Died December 22, 1865.
10	Columbus	1847	William B. Hubbard, Columbus	Died January 5, 1866.
11	Boston	1850	William B. Hubbard, Columbus	
12	Lexington	1853	William B. Hubbard, Columbus	
13	Hartford	1856	William B. Hubbard, Columbus	
14	Chicago	1859	Benjamin B. French, Washington	Died August 12, 1870.
15	New York	1862	Benjamin B. French, Washington	
16	Columbus	1865	Henry L. Palmer, Milwaukee	

17	St. Louis	1868	William S. Gardner, Newton, Mass	Died April 14, 1888.
18	Baltimore	1871	John Q. A. Fellows, New Orleans	
19	New Orleans	1874	James. H. Hopkins, Pittsburg	
20	Cleveland	1877	Vincent L. Hurlbut, Chicago	
21	Chicago	1880	Benjamin Dean, Boston	
22	San Francisco	1883	Robert E. Withers, Wytheville, Va.	
23	St. Louis	1886	Charles Roome, New York	Died June 28, 1890.
24	Washington	1889	John P. S. Gobin, Lebanon, Pa.	
25	Denver	1892	Hugh McCurdy, Corunna, Mich.	
26	Boston	1895		
27		1898		
28		1901		

THE ANCIENT ORDER OF THE TEMPLE.

Grand Masters from origin to the death of De Molai:

1	Hugh de Payen	Chosen	1118
2	Robert de Burgundy	"	1139
3	Everard de Barres	"	1147
4	Bernard de Amelai	"	1151
5	Bertrand de Blanquefort	"	1154
6	Andrew de Montbar	"	1165
7	Philip de Naplond	"	1169
8	Odon de St. Amand	"	1171

9	Arnold de Troye	”	1180
10	John Terrio	”	1185
11	Gerard Ridefort	”	1187
12	Robert de Sable	”	1191
13	Gilbert Gralius	”	1196
14	Philip de Plesseis	”	1201
15	William de Chartres	”	1217
16	Peter de Montaigu	”	1218
17	Armand de Perigord	”	1229
18	Herman de Petragrorius	”	1237
19	William de Rupefort	”	1244
20	William de Sonnac	”	1247
21	Reginald Vichier	”	1250
22	Thomas Berard	”	1257
23	William de Beaujeau	”	1274
24	Theobald de Gaudin	”	1291
25	James de Molai	”	1298

De Molai burned at the stake, March 18, 1314.

BANNERS OF THE ORDER OF THE TEMPLE.

The following are the official descriptions of these Banners:

"The GRAND STANDARD is of white woolen or silk stuff, six feet in height and five feet in width, made tripartite at the bottom, fastened at the top to the cross-bar by nine rings; in the center of the field a blood-red Passion Cross, over which is the motto, "*In hoc Signo Vinces*," and under, "*Non Nobis Domine! non Nobis, sed Nomini tuo da Gloriam!*" The Cross to be four feet high, and the upright and bar to be seven inches wide. On the top of the staff a gilded globe or ball, four inches in diameter, surmounted by the Patriarchal Cross, twelve inches in height. The Cross to be crimson, edged with gold."

GRAND STANDARD.

"The BEAUCEANT is of woolen or silk stuff, same form and dimensions as the Grand Standard, and suspended in the same manner. The upper half of this standard is black, the lower half white."

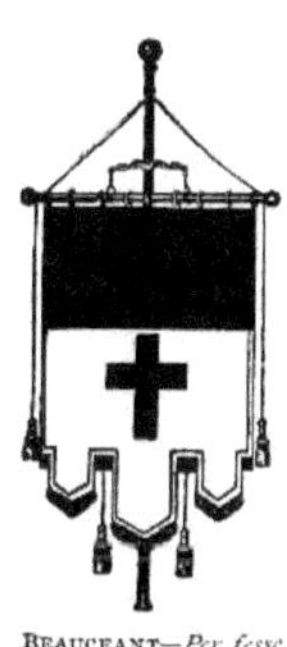

BEAUCEANT—*Per fesse.*

The Passion Cross is added in the drawing because the ancient Templars frequently so displayed it. And in that form they came to paint the Beauceant upon their kite-shaped Shields, as an armorial bearing.

Anciently the Beauceant was sometimes divided *per pale*, that is, perpendicularly, but generally it was divided *per fesse*, horizontally. The two forms here given were familiar to our ancient brethren.

The Beauceant was the battle flag of the Templars, and the *Vexillum Belli* of the Order was a white banner, on which was displayed, in full size, the "Red Cross of the Order." This standard was unfurled at the headquarters of the Grand Master during time of war, but the Beauceant was always carried into the battle. This standard was known as the "Red Cross War Banner of the Order," and the Beauceant as the "Battle Flag of the Order."

BEAUCEANT—*Per fesse.*

CROSSES OF THE ORDER OF THE TEMPLE,
UNDER THE JURISDICTION OF THE GRAND ENCAMPMENT.

SALEM.

CROSS OF SALEM.—This is worn by the Grand Master as the proper emblem of his office. It is borne before the Pope in procession, and is therefore called the Pontifical Cross. When in purple enamel, and edged with gold, it is the insignia of the Grand Master and of Past Grand Masters.

PATRIARCHAL.

PATRIARCHAL CROSS.—This Cross when in purple enamel, and edged with gold, is the insignia of all officers of the Grand Encampment below the Grand Master.

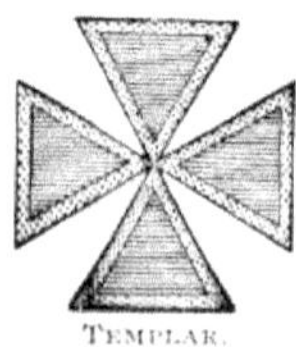

TEMPLAR.

TEMPLAR CROSS.—This Cross is formed of four equilateral triangles joined at the apices, and is called the Cross patée. It is the insignia of the officers of a Grand Commandery.

It is insisted upon by learned antiquarians that this is the Red Cross of the Order which the ancient Templars wore. That Cross is described as of "equal limbs, somewhat wider and somewhat concave at the ends, heraldically called patée." The "Ancient Red," here given, illustrates that Cross, and the author of this Monitor is inclined to accept it in preference to the form adopted by the Grand Encampment of the United States. This Cross was given the Templars by Pope Eugenius, and some think the Cross he gave them had its lower limb longer than the others, as in the Passion Cross.

PASSION.

PASSION CROSS.—When in red enamel, and edged with gold, the Passion Cross is the insignia of a Commander of a Commandery. This Cross appears on the Grand Standard of the Order in the United States.

MALTA.

CROSS OF MALTA.—This Cross has not been adopted as insignia by the Grand Encampment. It is of white enamel, and edged with gold, and formed into eight points, as above, to represent the eight *langes* into which the Hospitalers (Knights of Malta) were divided.

THE PARAPHERNALIA OF A COMMANDERY OF KNIGHTS TEMPLAR.

1. A TRIANGLE.—This is a triangular Table, of the height of thirty-two inches, and with sides not less than six feet in length. It may be covered with black velvet, and be draped with silver-fringed valance.

2. THE CHAMBER.—This room to be entirely in black, even. to the floor.

3. THE SEPULCHRE.—The Chamber may be utilized as the Sepulchre by suspending a curtain, with a proper painting thereon, from the ceiling, so as to conceal, at the proper time, the equipments of the Chamber proper.

4. ASCENSION.—Lanterns are becoming popular, but a movable Scene is much to be preferred.

5. Altar, for Prelate's use in Prelate's Hall.

6. Lectern, for Prelate's use in Asylum.

7. Robe, Mitre, Cross, and Crozier, for Prelate.

8. Pilgrim's Garb, Sandals, Staff, and Scrip.

9. Sword and Buckler.

10. Robes and Hats, for Hermits.

11. Three Tents, changeable to Huts.

12. White Robe for Penitential Year.

13. Taper for the P. P.

14. Equipments for Triangle and the Chamber.

These are necessary to the proper rendition of the ceremonies of the Order of the Temple. It is not sufficient excuse for the absence of any of them that the funds of the Commandery do not permit their purchase. A Commandery unable to provide itself with a comfortable Asylum, and the proper equipments, should not try to exist. Templarism is a luxury, and should be looked upon as an expensive one by those seeking to establish and maintain a Commandery.

THE OFFICERS OF A COMMANDERY OF KNIGHTS TEMPLAR.

Eminent Commander	EC	1
Generalissimo	G	2
Captain General	CG	3
Excellent Prelate	P	4
Senior Warden	SW	5
Junior Warden	JW	6
Treasurer	Tr	7
Recorder	Rec	8
Standard Bearer	StB	9
Sword Bearer	Sw B	10
Warder	W	11
Sentinel	Sen	12
Guards (who are also Hermits)	Gd	13

The officers of a Commandery should wear black clothing, and during the conferring of the Orders should be fully equipped as Knights Templar. The Prelate should wear the regulation Robes during the entire ceremonials.

The members of a Commandery should wear black clothing. Light clothing is not in harmony with the Order of the Temple, nor is it becoming under the regulation uniform.

The Guards must be fully equipped as Knights Templar, and never appear on duty in fatigue uniform.

When the Guards put on dark robes over their Templar equipments, and replace their chapeaux with soft hats, they become Hermits. The Hermits, thus robed, should represent aged men.

When the Pilgrimage ends the Hermits doff their robes, and they are in full Templar equipments as soon as they put on their chapeaux.

TO OPEN A COMMANDERY.

KNIGHTS TEMPLAR begin the duties of their Asylums with quiet manner and subdued spirit. At the conclusion there should be only pathetic memories of solemn ceremonials. Levity, loud speech, military drill, are not to be encouraged in the ceremonies of Knighthood.

The Asylum is suitably arrayed under the direction of the Captain General, who is responsible to the Commander that everything is in readiness, both for the transaction of business and the reception of candidates.

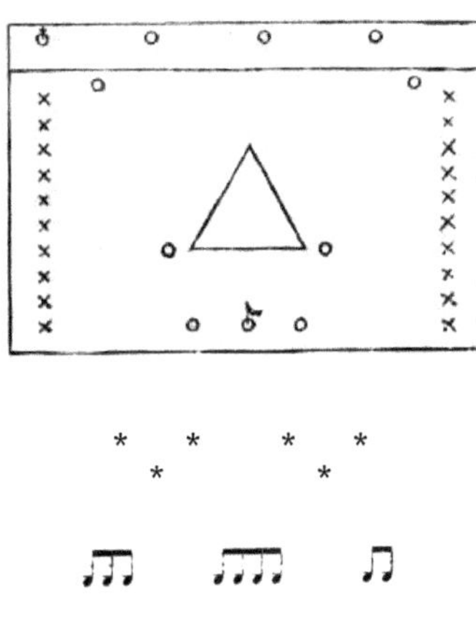

RECEPTION OF EMINENT COMMANDER.

Each Jurisdiction will conduct this ceremonial according to the Tactics it may have adopted.

COMMUNICATIONS.

ACROSS THE LINES.— * * *

This ceremony admits of very little variation. Nevertheless the Grand Encampment permits each Grand Jurisdiction to conduct the same according to the Tactics it may have adopted for its government.

The ceremony should be conducted with dignity and precision. A knowledge of the use of the sword is necessary to that dignity and precision; therefore the Sword Exercise should not be neglected by the Commanderies.

Commanders will discover a greater precision when the numbers are called by the Captain General.

Through the Lines.—Care is necessary to make this ceremony effective.

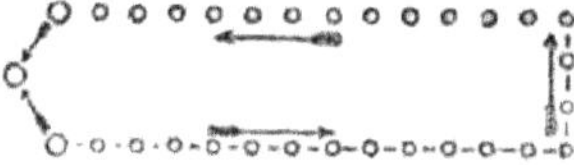

Through Both Lines Simultaneously.—

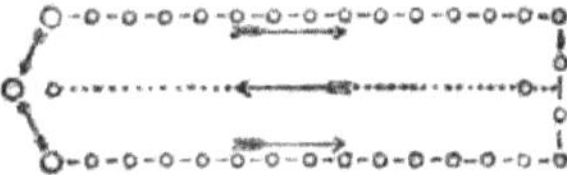

FIRST ANNUNCIATION.

Behold, a virgin shall be with child, and shall bring forth a son, and they shall call his name (or his name shall be called) Emmanuel, which being interpreted is, God With Us. Matt. i: 23.

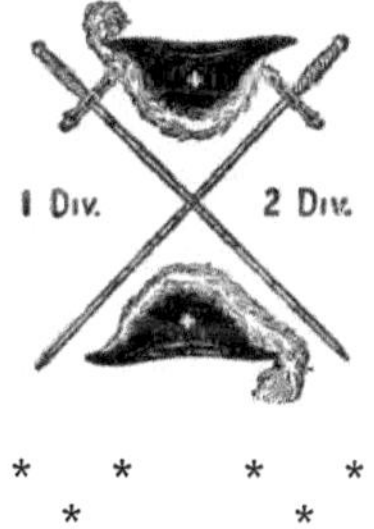

*   *   *   *
*   *

INSPECTION AND REVIEW,

If the Commander should desire to have Inspection and Review he will order them here. They will be conducted according to the Tactics of the Jurisdiction.

PRAYER.

ALMIGHTY and Most Merciful Father, send down upon us at this time the dew of thy heavenly grace; forgive our many transgressions; refresh us with the sweetness of thy love, and enrich our hearts with patience and hope. May we bear each other's burdens here, and may we live together hereafter in that blessed kingdom to which thy glorified Son will welcome his disciples. And to thy great and matchless Name shall be all the glory through Jesus Christ, Emmanuel. AMEN.

Our Father which art in heaven, Hallowed be thy name. Thy kingdom come. Thy will be done in earth, as *it is* in heaven. Give us this day our daily bread. And forgive us our debts, as we forgive our debtors.

And lead us not into temptation, but deliver us from evil: For thine is the kingdom, and the power; and the glory, forever. AMEN.

Other devotional exercises may occur at this point in the opening.

*   *   *   *
*   *

The S—s should be given by the entire Commandery, hence it is proper to give them *after* the Triangle is reduced.

REHEARSAL OF DUTIES.

Each officer being in his station, it is eminently fit and proper that he should rehearse aloud the duties that appertain to his office. He should do so in an attitude of dignified respect.

When an officer is addressed he will arise, and salute as directed in the Ritual. After he has replied he will stand fast until the conclusion of the opening ceremonial, or until addressed again.

*   *   *   *
*   *

SENTINEL INFORMED.

♫   ♫♫   ♪

IN SHORT FORM.

A Commandery should always be opened in Full Form. What is worth doing at all is worth doing well. Commanders should not gratify a mere desire to shirk formality. But if circumstances render abbreviation imperatively necessary, then there is a Form that MUST be observed. Under no circumstances shall less than that Essential Form be observed. Commanders will not overlook that Ritual requirement.

THE WORK.

The Asylum in suitable array; the Guards ready to take their stations; the Escort selected and conveniently seated; the Chambers properly equipped, and the Questions on the pedestal of the Commander. The reception of a Candidate begins.

*   *   *   *
*   *

During the period that immediately succeeded the Crusades a civil Knight made a vow to visit the Sepulchre of his Lord and

Master. Attracted by the chivalrous deeds of the Templars,—for their deeds of charity and pure beneficence had spread their fame both far and wide,—he sought admission to their ranks, the better to fulfill his vow.

The Commander of the House of the Temple to which he made application, finding that he came "under the tongue of good report," and that he was upright in character and moral of conduct, was moved to grant his prayer, but as a trial of his worthiness to be enrolled among the members of the Valiant and Magnanimous Order of the Temple enjoined upon him Seven Years of Preparation. These began with an unarmed pilgrimage towards the Holy Sepulchre.

*   *   *   *
*   *

THE CHAMBER.

The first impressions are almost indelible. How important that they should be solemnized by proper discourse in the sombre surroundings of Reflection.

*   *   *   *
*   *

Sincerity of desire and purity of intention are absolutely necessary to the beginning of a pilgrimage to the Shrine of Emmanuel.

THE ASYLUM.

♫ ♬ ♪

The Report includes the necessary answers, and the avouchment of the sincerity of desire, and the purity of motive. This
made, the Seven Years of Preparation begin.

*   *   *   *
*   *

THE PILGRIMAGE.

Three years were passed by the petitioning civil
Knight in his weary, unarmed pilgrimage, mostly
in a friendly country, in which he received from
pious Hermits bread and water; coarse diet, but
such as he stood sadly in need of.

From these pious anchorites he also received
lessons of comfort and consolation.

Day after day the manhood of this gallant Knight asserted itself, and he yearned to cast off the pilgrim's garb and take up the
sword in defense of his fellow pilgrims *en route* to the Holy
Shrine. Thus yearning and pleading with his Templar escort, he
reached, at the end of three years, another House of the Templars.

*   *   *   *
*   *

FIRST HERMIT.—

Let the brother of low degree rejoice in that he is exalted.

Come unto me, all ye that labor and are heavy laden, and I will give you rest.

Christ also suffered for us, leaving us an example, that ye should follow his steps.

For ye were as sheep going astray; but are now returned unto the Shepherd and Bishop of your souls. Let brotherly love continue.

* * * *
* *

SECOND HERMIT.—

To do good and to communicate forget not: for with such sacrifices God is well pleased.

Be not forgetful to entertain strangers: for thereby some have entertained angels unawares.

Remember them that are in bonds, as bound with them; and them which suffer adversity, as being yourselves also in the body.

Let us not be weary in well doing: for in due season we shall reap, if we faint not.

* * * *
* *

THIRD HERMIT.—

Charity shall cover the multitude of sins.

If a brother or sister be naked, and destitute of daily food, and one of you say unto them, Depart in peace, be ye warmed and filled; notwithstanding ye give them not those things which are needful to the body; what doth it profit?

Be thou faithful unto death, and I will give thee a crown of life.

*   *   *   *
*   *

Three years of his Preparation being ended, another House of the Templars was reached.

SECOND HOUSE OF THE TEMPLARS.

The escort pleaded that the four remaining years might be devoted to deeds of more exalted usefulness. He vouched for the sincerity of the suppliant.

The prayer of the suppliant was granted, and he was admitted to the Vows.

* * * *
* *

The laying aside of the pilgrim's garb, and the sandals, staff, and scrip, was followed by the taking up of the sword and buckler, and the consecrating of the sword to the noblest of uses.

THE VOW.

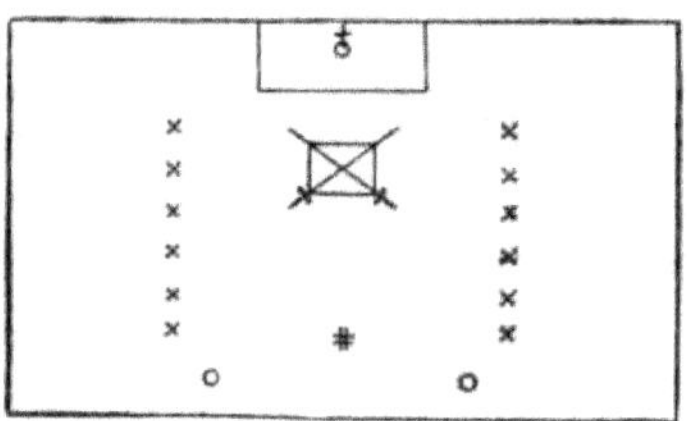

* * * *
* *

The gallant Knight sallied forth, armed with sword and buckler, ready to defend the Christian religion, or any pilgrim, or devotee, whether the same should be innocent maiden, destitute widow, or helpless orphan. Onward he pressed, with fortitude undaunted, accepting the duty of clothing the naked, feeding the hungry, and binding up the wounds of the afflicted; thus giving ample proof that he was worthy of drawing the sword he had so solemnly consecrated.

Pride and selfishness came with the accomplishment of valorous deeds, and he began to yearn for those honors and rewards that awaited the valiant Knights Templar, whom he found guarding the dangerous passes. No rewards, and no permanent honors awaited unorganized warfare. He had traveled on during three years with patience and perseverance, and during the three years last past he had given ample proofs of his courage and constancy. "Why should I longer be preparing?" he asked of his warrior escort. While he thus pleaded six years of his Preparation were accomplished, and they reached a third House of the Templars. Then he pleaded with his Templar companion to beseech the Commander of that House to remit the remaining year of his Preparation.

Naturally his Templar companion hesitated to make such a request, and carefully interrogated his ward. At last it was agreed that if the suppliant could declare in truth and soberness that his heart was right with man, and before God, he would vouch for him to the Commander, and present his petition for remission.

THIRD HOUSE OF THE TEMPLARS.

There is a legend told beyond seas to this effect: When the Papacy decided to suppress the Templars it sent out spies to apply to the Order as neophytes, and if admitted, to betray the secrets to the Church. Absolution from vows so taken was promised.

The Templars sought to protect themselves from treason of every kind, and it is said that when a neophyte was not absolutely above suspicion the Commander directed that he be tested by a solemn imprecation, accompanied by a draft from a cup containing blood taken from his veins at that moment, and mingled with wine. This in imitation of the blood and water that flowed from the Saviour's side.

That ceremony was truly appalling in those days of superstition; it would have small influence were it practiced in this age of intelligence.

THE ENTRANCE.

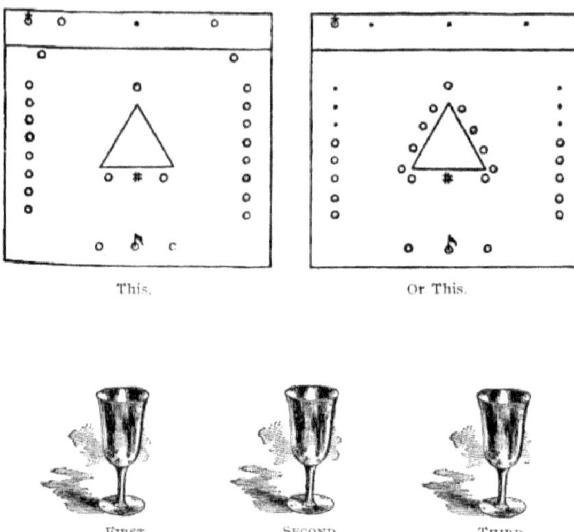

1. Fear God and keep his commandments.

2. Embalm in acts of charity, and deeds of pure beneficence.

3. Yield up life rather than forfeit integrity.

FIRST LESSON.—Then one of the twelve, called Judas Iscariot, went unto the chief priests,

And said *unto them*, what will ye give me, and I will deliver him unto you? And they covenanted with him for thirty pieces of silver.

And from that time he sought opportunity to betray him.

Now, the first *day* of the *feast of* unleavened bread the disciples came to Jesus, saying unto him, Where wilt thou that we prepare for thee to eat the passover?

And he said, Go into the city to such a man, and say unto him, The Master saith, My time is at hand; I will keep the passover at thy house with my disciples.

And the disciples did as Jesus had appointed them; and they made ready the passover. Now when the even was come, he sat down with the twelve.

And as they did eat, he said, Verily I say unto you, that one of you shall betray me.

And they were exceeding sorrowful, and began every one of them to say unto him, Lord, is it I?

And he answered and said, He that dippeth *his* hand with me in the dish, the same shall betray me.

The Son of man goeth as it is written of him: but woe unto that man by whom the Son of man is betrayed! it had been good for that man if he had not been born. Then Judas, which betrayed him, answered and said, Master, is it I? He said unto him, Thou hast said. Matt. xxvi: 14-25.

The number of the Apostles of our Saviour while on earth was Twelve. One of them betrayed his Lord and Master. His light was extinguished as the symbol of direst condemnation.

The extinguishment of light was the ancient symbol of the direst punishment for crime. Ezekiel xxxii: 7, says: "And when I shall put thee out (extinguish), I will cover the heaven, and make the stars thereof dark." How forcibly is this thought brought to the mind of the neophyte in this ceremonial.

SECOND LESSON.—Then cometh Jesus with them unto a place called Gethsemane, and saith unto the disciples, Sit ye here, while I go and pray yonder.

And he took with him Peter and the two sons of Zebedee, and began to be sorrowful and very heavy.

Then saith he unto them, My soul is exceeding sorrowful, even unto death: tarry ye here, and watch with me.
And he went a little farther, and fell on his face, and prayed, saying, O my Father, if it be possible, let this cup pass from me: nevertheless, not as I will, but as thou *wilt.*

And he cometh unto the disciples, and findeth them asleep, and saith unto Peter, What, could ye not watch with me one hour?

The lowering of the l—s alludes to the allegory related by Ezekiel, in regard to covering the heavens, and making the stars thereof dark.

Watch and pray, that ye enter not into temptation: the spirit indeed *is* willing, but the flesh *is* weak.

He went away again the second time, and prayed, saying, O my Father, if this cup may not pass away from me, except I drink it, thy will be done.

And he came and found them asleep again: for their eyes were heavy.

And he left them, and went away again, and prayed the third
time, saying the same words.

Then cometh he to his disciples, and saith unto them, Sleep on
now, and take *your* rest: behold, the hour is at hand, and the
Son of man is betrayed into the hands of sinners.

Rise, let us be going: behold, he is at hand that Both betray
me.

And while he yet spake, lo, Judas, one of the twelve, came, and
with him a great multitude with swords and staves, from the
chief priests and elders of the people.

Now he that betrayed him gave them a sign, saying, Whomsoever
I shall kiss, that same is he: hold him fast.

And forthwith he came to Jesus, and said, Hail, Master; and
kissed him. Matt. xxvi: 41-49.

*   *   *   *
*   *

Uncovering with great solemnity, and with soft music, desirable.

*   *   *   *
*   *

It is the creed of the Templar that all the hopes of his poor
perishing body rest upon the truths revealed in the Word of
God; and that amid all the vicissitudes of life an unswerving
faith in those truths can alone afford him that strong consolation which the world can neither give nor take away.

*   *   *   *
*   *

Third Lesson.— * * *

When Pilate saw that he could prevail nothing, but *that* rather a tumult was made, he took water, and washed *his* hands before the multitude, saying, I am innocent of the blood of this just person: see ye *to it.*

Then answered all the people, and said, His blood *be* on us, and on our children.

Then released he Barabbas unto them: and when he had scourged Jesus, he delivered *him* to be crucified.

Then the soldiers of the governor took Jesus into the common hall, and gathered unto him the whole band *of soldiers.*

And they stripped him, and put on him a scarlet robe.
And when they had platted a crown of thorns, they put *it* upon his head, and a reed in his right hand: and they bowed the knee before him, and mocked him, saying, Hail, King of the Jews!

And they spit upon him, and took the reed, and smote him on the head.

And after that they had mocked him, they took the robe off from him, and put his own raiment on him, and led him away to crucify *him.*

And as they came out, they found a man of Cyrene, Simon by name: him they compelled to bear his cross.

And when they were come unto a place called Golgotha, that is to say, a place of a skull.

They gave him vinegar to drink, mingled with gall: and when he had tasted *thereof,* he would not drink.

And they crucified him, and parted his garments, casting lots: that it might be fulfilled which was spoken by the prophet, They parted my garments among them, and upon my vesture did they cast lots.

And sitting down, they watched him there;
And set up over his head his accusation written, THIS IS JESUS, THE KING OF THE JEWS. Matt. xxvii: 24- 37.

FOURTH.

*　　*　　*　　*
　*　　　　*

Let each so wear the cross as to be deemed worthy to wear the crown.

*　　*　　*　　*
　*　　　　*

The ecclesiastical legend that Simon of Cyrene was the "early friend and companion of our Saviour," and that "he fell a martyr to his faith," is not accepted by the Order of the Temple. It is probable that Simon was a chance spectator of the procession to Calvary, and that the Romans, scorning to burden themselves with the cross of execution, impressed this foreigner, and forced him to bear the fatal tree after Jesus had fallen under its weight. There appears to be some proof that Simon afterwards became a member of the Christian community.

*　　*　　*　　*
　*　　　　*

Well might the suppliant, now more haughty than humble, be required to meditate upon the uncertainty of all things earthly.

O death! who shall resist thy imperious mandate; who shall bid thee defiance!

*　　*　　*　　*
*　　　　*

The petitioning Knight was now required to devote the remaining year of Preparation to penitence and self-abnegation. Clothed in an emblem of innocence, and bearing symbols of Faith and Humility, he was enjoined to so let his light shine before men that they might glorify his Father which is in heaven.

*　　*　　*　　*
*　　　　*

"WHERE THE LORD LAY."

*　　*　　*　　*
*　　　　*

In the end of the sabbath, as it began to dawn toward the first *day* of the week, came Mary Magdalene and the other Mary to see the sepulchre. And, behold, there was a great earthquake: for the angel of the Lord descended from heaven, and came and rolled back the stone from the door, and sat upon it. His countenance was like lightning, and his raiment white as snow: And for fear of him the keepers did shake, and became as dead men.

And the angel answered and said unto the women, Fear not ye: for I know that ye seek Jesus, which was crucified. He is not here: for he is risen, as he said. Come, see the place where the Lord lay. Matt. xxviii: i-6.

*   *   *   *
*   *

And as it is appointed unto men once to die, but after this the judgment: So Christ was once offered to bear the, sins of many; and unto them that look for him shall he appear the second time without sin unto salvation. Heb. ix: 27, 28.

And go quickly, and tell his disciples that he is risen from the dead; and, behold, he goeth before you into Galilee; there shall ye see him: lo, I have told you.

And they departed quickly from the sepulchre with fear and great joy; and did run to bring his disciples word. And as they went to tell his disciples, behold, Jesus met them, saying, All hail. And they came and held him by the feet, and worshipped him. Then said Jesus unto them, Be not afraid: go tell my brethren that they go into Galilee, and there shall they see me. Matt. xxviii: 7-10.

*   *   *   *
*   *

TOWARDS BETHANY.

*   *   *   *
*   *

I am the resurrection, and the life: he that believeth in me, though he were dead, yet shall he live. And whosoever liveth and believeth in me shall never die. John xi: 25, 26.

And he led them out as far as to Bethany, and he lifted up his hands, and blessed them. And it came to pass, while he blessed them, he was parted from them, and carried up into heaven. Luke xxiv: 50, 51.

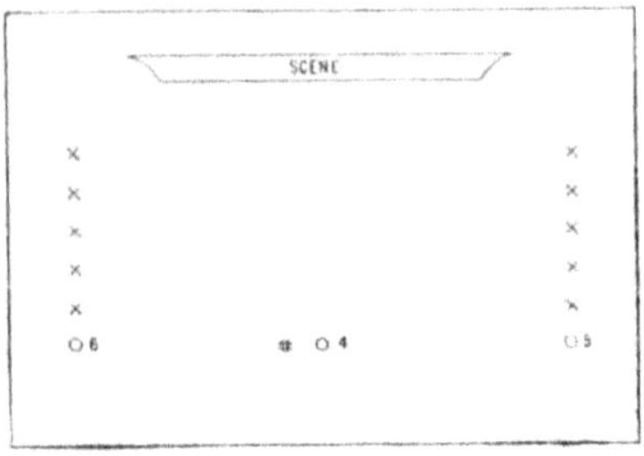

HYMNS.

AIR, *Old Hundred*. L. M.

The rising God forsakes the tomb!
Up to his Father's court he flies;
Cherubic legions guard him home,
And shout him welcome to the skies.

Break off your tears, ye saints, and tell
How high our great deliv'rer reigns,
Sing how he spoil'd the hosts of hell,
And led the tyrant, death, in chains.

AIR, *Hendon*. 7s.

Lo! the heavens its Lord receives,
Yet he loves the earth he leaves;
Though returning to his throne,
Still he calls mankind his own.

Lord, though parted from our
Far above the starry height, sight,
Grant our hearts may thither rise,
Seeking thee above the skies.

CLOSE OF SEVEN YEARS OF PREPARATION.

One mode of entrance is thus accomplished. Silence reigns.

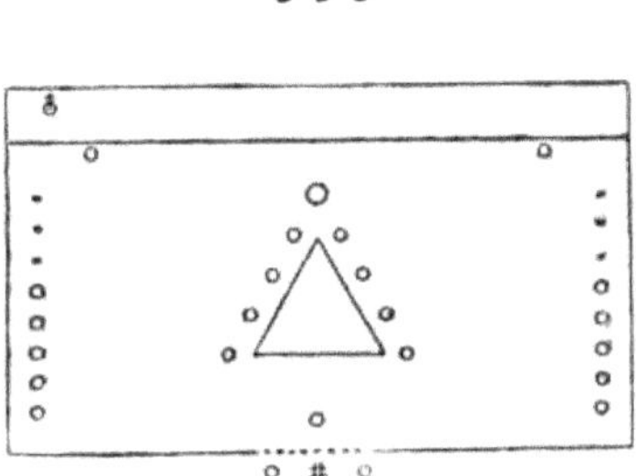

Another mode of entrance is thus secured. Silence reigns.

*   *   *   *
     *   *

Plaintive music touches the heart of the neophyte while gazing at the solemn observance of Prayer and Meditation. The memorial of the betrayal before him, he laments the disloyalty of the one so fully trusted. Thrilled by the surroundings, he craves admission, that he, too, might seal his faith, never to be renounced.

*   *   *   *
     *   *

His allotted year of Penitence had ended, but his need of penitence had not, since all men err, and erring need repentance.

*   *   *   *
     *   *

Alas! men are born to die! Can man be too frequently reminded of this.

*   *   *   *
    *   *

Why should the humble follower of Jesus loiter in his foot-
steps, or fall by the wayside? Is not Jesus sufficient? He is, and
should temptation assail; should misfortune befall; should all the
world seem to forsake the true Soldier of Christ, he will nevertheless remain faithful to his vows. And he will never bring disgrace upon himself, or reproach upon the name of Him under
whose banner he has enlisted.

*   *   *   *
    *   *

The casting of lots was an ancient custom, and is frequently
mentioned in the Scriptures. Several methods of casting the lots
were practiced. Solomon says, Proverbs xvi: 33, "The lot is cast
into the lap," That is, the pebble is cast into the *bechif,*—lap, or
bottom of an urn. Perhaps a literal rendering of the verse quoted
above will cast some light on that one method.

"In a lot-vase the lots are shaken in all directions; nevertheless,
from the Lord is their whole decision,—judgment."

The Order of the Temple has adopted a method of "casting
lots" peculiar to itself.

And in those days Peter stood up in the midst of the disciples, and said, (the number of names together were about an hundred and twenty.)

Men *and* brethren, the scripture must needs have been fulfilled, which the Holy Ghost by the mouth of David spake before concerning Judas, which was guide to them that took Jesus.

For he was numbered with us, and had obtained part of this ministry.

Now this man purchased a field with the reward of iniquity; and falling headlong, he burst asunder in the midst, and all his bowels gushed out.

And it was known unto all the dwellers at Jerusalem; insomuch as that field is called in their proper tongue, Aceldama, that is to say, The field of blood.

For it is written in the book of Psalms, Let his habitation be desolate, and let no man dwell therein: and his bishopric let another take.

Wherefore of these men which have companied with us all the time that the Lord Jesus went in and out among us. Beginning from the baptism of John, unto that same day that he was taken up from us, must one be ordained to be a witness with us of his resurrection.

And they appointed two, Joseph called Barsabas, who was surnamed Justus, and Matthias. And they prayed, and said, Thou, Lord, which knowest the hearts of all *men*, show whether of these two thou hast chosen, that he may take part of this ministry and apostleship, from which Judas by transgression fell, that he might go to his own place.

And they gave forth their lots; and the lot fell upon Matthias; and he was numbered with the eleven apostles. Acts i: 15-26.

*   *   *   *
*   *

When Judas betrayed his Lord and Master his light became darkness in the college of Apostles. When the divine wisdom selected Matthias to fill the vacancy that light was restored. Sin puts out the divine light in the heart, but it is restored when the heart elects to serve the Master unto death.

*   *   *   *
*   *

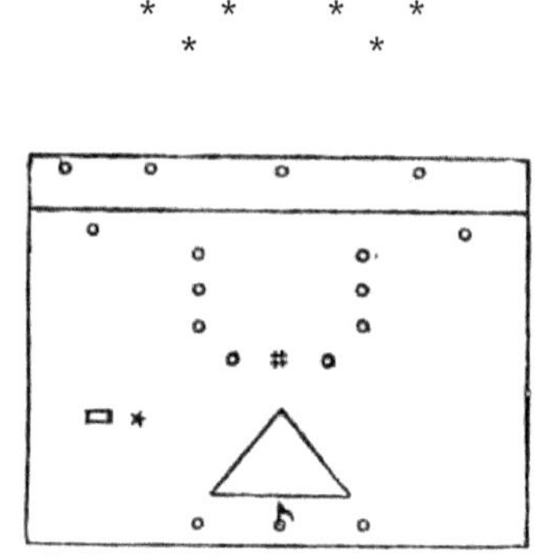

* A small table on which is the armor of the candidate.

It was the custom of the Grand Master to put his arm about the neck of the initiate, and thus make him a Templar. Anciently kings conferred knighthood in the same way.

The word Accolade is front *ad*, to, and *collum*, the neck. The embrace has long passed out of use, and the single blow on the candidate's left shoulder with the blade of the sword has been adopted.

It is generally held that the one blow with the blade of the Sword had its origin in the single blow which the slave of the Romans received at his manumission.

*   *   *   *
*   *

THE BALDRIC.

Such Grand Commanderies as have discarded the Baldric are excused from the ceremony of its investiture.

*   *   *   *
*   *

THE SWORD.

The investiture of the Sword is an imposing and an imperative ceremonial.

*   *   *   *
*   *

THE SPUR.

The investiture of the Spur is left to the discretion of the Grand Commanderies, and of Commanders where Grand Commanderies have taken no action thereon.

* *   *   *
*   *

MEANS OF RECOGNITION.

* *   *   *
*   *

THE BANNERS.

There are two which belong to the Order of the Temple at this time. They are the Grand Standard and the Beauceant.

The Grand Standard is of blue field, five by six feet, and made tripartite at the bottom. Over the blood- red Passion Cross in the center is the Motto of the Order, "*In Hoc Signo Vinces.*" Beneath the Cross is the ancient Templar motto, "*Non nobis Domine; non nobis, sed Nomini tuo da Gloriam.*"

The Beauceant is of the same form and dimensions as the Grand Standard. The upper half of this Banner is black, and the lower half is white.

When the Templar looks upon the GRAND STANDARD he is admonished to so live and serve the Master that having passed through the portals of the grave he may receive from his hand the Crown of Victory, while exclaiming, "NOT UNTO US, O LORD; NOT UNTO US, BUT UNTO THY NAME BE THE GLORY."

THE BEAUCEANT.—This was the Battle Flag of the ancient Templars. It is half black and half white; signifying that these Christian warriors were fair and favorable to the friends of Christ, but dark and terrible to his enemies.

Sometimes this Banner was divided per pale, that is, perpendicularly, but most frequently per fesse, that is, horizontally, the upper half always black.

The red Passion Cross was sometimes on the white, but never on the black. Color upon color would be false heraldry. The cry of the Templars was, "Au Bausant for the Temple," but what that cry really meant is not understood to-day.

The ancient Templars frequently painted the Beauceant upon their kite-shaped shields, as an armorial bearing. It was said to betoken Innocence, Death and Martyrdom.

*   *   *   *
*   *

HISTORICAL LECTURE.

During the period that succeeded the Crusades a civil Knight made a vow to visit the sepulchre of his Lord and Master. Attracted by the chivalrous deeds of the Knights Templar,—for their deeds of charity and pure beneficence had spread their fame both far and wide,—he sought admission to their ranks, the better to fulfill that vow.

The Prior of the Templars to whom he made his application being satisfied with the report made thereon as to the uprightness of character of the applicant, was moved to grant the prayer of his petition, but as a trial of his worthiness to be enrolled among the members of the valiant and magnanimous Order of the Temple, he enjoined upon him Seven Years of Preparation. These began with an unarmed pilgrimage in the direction of the Holy Shrine. An escort was furnished to guide and protect him. And so, without sword or buckler, and forbidden to do acts unbecoming an humble pilgrim, the journey began. To a man of warlike spirit and chivalrous nature such pilgrimage was indeed a trial of patience and perseverance.

Three years were passed in this weary way, mostly in a friendly country, in which the pilgrim received from pious anchorites bread and water, as well as lessons of comfort and consolation. But day after day his manhood asserted itself with accumulating vigor, when he beheld indignities offered not only to himself, but to other helpless pilgrims—many of them delicate women. Then he yearned to cast off the garb of a pilgrim, and, laying aside the staff, to grasp the sword and perform deeds of more exalted usefulness. While pleading with his devoted escort for the gratification of his manly ambition he reached a House of the Templars. Three years of his Preparation had passed, and the zealous Knight implored his escort to crave the permission of the Prior to devote the four remaining years to deeds of more exalted usefulness.

The escort was moved by his entreaties, vouched for him to the Prior that he had performed full three years of Preparation, made his burning desires known, and cordially recommended him to official favor. The avouchment of his escort secured the favorable consideration of the Prior, who, after putting him under vows, granted him permission to take up sword and buckler, and go forth under escort of a Templar warrior, manfully wielding his sword in the defense of innocent maidens, destitute widows, helpless orphans and the Christian religion. And such a warfare was indeed a trial of his constancy and courage.

As a warrior this gallant Knight pressed forward with fortitude undaunted, giving ample proof to his warrior escort that he was worthy to draw the sword in the cause to which he had consecrated it. But his deeds of valor soon created in him an ardent desire to be admitted to where honors and rewards await the results of valor and chivalry. He met armed Templars gallantly defending the dangerous passes of his route, and he yearned to be admitted to their ranks.

Three years more passed in this vigorous warfare, and at the close of the third year he reached another House of the Templars. Then he besought his warrior guide to implore the Prior to remit the remaining year of his Preparation.

The warrior escort presented the petition to the Prior, vouched for the valor, courage and constancy of the petitioner, and that he had faithfully performed six of his seven years of Preparation, and even recommended that the remission asked for be granted, if it should so please the Prior. And though the Prior was moved by the recital of the deeds of valor wrought by the petitioner, and by the history of his courage and constancy, he could not shorten the time of Preparation laid on him at the beginning.

Moreover, he feared that the memory of those acts of valor filled his heart with pride, and that self- confidence had supplanted an humble reliance upon the strong arm of the Master. He therefore commanded the petitioner to devote the remaining year of Preparation to penitence, as a trial of his faith and humility.

With the accomplishment of the penitential year the term of preparation ended, and the devoted neophyte was permitted to seal his faith and enlist under the banner of the Temple and of Emmanuel.

At the death of De Molai the ancient Order of the Temple was suppressed and its members dispersed. The warlike spirit that gave it birth has passed away, but in this modern Order of the Temple there remains a spirit of refined and moral chivalry which should prompt all of its members to be ever ready to defend the weak, the innocent, the helpless and the oppressed; and in a brother's cause to do all that may be demanded by manhood and fraternity.

THE CHARGE.

The following Charge may be omitted and the Historical Lecture delivered instead. Or both may be omitted in the discretion of the Commander.

Sir Knight, having passed through the several degrees of our ancient and honorable institution, we bid you a hearty welcome to all our rights and privileges, even to that disinterested friendship and unbounded hospitality which ever has, and we hope and trust ever will, continue to adorn, distinguish and characterize this noble Order.

It will henceforth become your duty to assist, protect and defend the weary, wayworn traveler who finds the heights of fortune inaccessible, and the thorny paths of life broken, adverse and forlorn,—to succor, defend and protect the *innocent*, the *distressed* and the *helpless*, ever standing forth as a champion to espouse the cause of the *Christian Religion*.

You are to inculcate, enforce and practice virtue; and amid all the temptations which surround you, never to be drawn aside from the path oaf duty, or forgetful of those due guards and passwords, which are necessary to be had in perpetual remembrance; and while one hand is wielding the Sword for the defense of your Companion in danger, let the other grasp the mystic Trowel, and widely diffuse the genuine cement of Brotherly Love and Friendship.

Should calumny assail the character of a Brother Sir Knight, recollect that you are to step forth and vindicate his good name, and assist him on all lawful occasions. Should assailants ever attempt your honor, interest or happiness, remember, also, that you have the counsel and support of your brethren, whose mystic Swords, combining the virtues of Faith, Hope and Charity, with *Justice*, *Fortitude* and *Mercy*, will leap from their scabbards in defense of your just rights, and insure you a glorious triumph over all your enemies.

On this occasion permit me, Sir Knight, to remind you of our mutual engagements, our reciprocal ties; for whatever may be your situation or rank in life, you may find those in similar stations, who have dignified themselves and been useful to mankind. You are, therefore, called upon to discharge all your duties with fidelity and patience, whether in the *Field*, in the *Senate*, on the *Bench*, at the *Bar*, or at the *Holy Altar*. Whether you are placed upon the highest pinnacle of worldly grandeur, or glide into the humble vale of obscurity, unnoticed, save by a few, it matters not; for a few rolling suns will close the scene, when naught but holiness will serve as a sure passport to gain admission into that REST prepared from the foundation of the world.

If you see a Brother bending under the cross of adversity and disappointment, look not idly on, neither pass by on the other side, but fly to his relief. If he be deceived, tell him the *Truth*; if he be calumniated, vindicate his cause; for, although he may have erred, still recollect that indiscretion in him should never destroy humanity in you.

Finally, Sir Knight, as *memento mori* is deeply engraved on all sublunary enjoyments, let us ever be found in the habiliments of righteousness, traversing the straight path of rectitude, virtue and true holiness; so that, having discharged our duty here below, performed the pilgrimage of life, burst the bands of mortality, passed over the Jordan of death and safely landed on the broad shore of eternity, there, in the presence of myriads of attending angels, we may be greeted as brethren, received into the arms of the BLESSED EMMANUEL, and forever made to participate in his HEAVENLY KINGDOM.

TO CLOSE THE COMMANDERY.

THE Commander directs that the same precautionary steps be taken previous to the ceremony of Closing.

* * * *
* *

PRAYER.

The Prelate will lead in the Lord's Prayer, after which he will pronounce this, or some other Benediction:

"The grace of our Lord Jesus Christ be with you. Amen."

* * * *
* *

A RITUALISTIC COMMENTARY.

"The adversaries of Judah and Benjamin heard that the children of the captivity builded the temple unto the Lord God of Israel." Ezra iv: 1.

The "adversaries" are enumerated in verses 7, 8 and 9. The territory assigned to Judah was about forty- five miles long and fifty miles wide, and extended from the Jordan to the Mediterranean. The territory assigned to Benjamin was about twenty-six miles long and twelve miles wide. It extended from the Jordan to seven miles west of Jerusalem.

These were the oldest and the youngest sons of Jacob, and they fell heir to Jerusalem, the Temple, and the glories of the Mosaic traditions, on the secession of the Ten Tribes under Rehoboam. Judah means "the praise of the Lord;" Benjamin means "the son of the right hand."

"And they shall call his name Emmanuel, which being interpreted is, God with us." Matt. i: 23. "Behold, a virgin shall conceive, and bear a son, and shall call his name Immanuel." Isaiah vii: 54.

Emmanuel is the Greek form of the Hebrew Immanuel. Ahaz is informed of the birth of Messiah by Isaiah, and Matthew says this prophecy was accomplished in the birth of Christ.

It was in its Greek form that the word was familiar to the Templars of old, as well as of to-day. "And thou shalt call his name Jesus: for he shall save his people from their sins." Matt. i: 21.

Jesus is the Greek form of the Hebrew Joshua, or Jeshua, which is a contraction of Jehoshua, (Numbers xiii: 16.) Its literal meaning is "he of Jehovah," and we define it as "Saviour." Jesus Christ means " Anointed Saviour." As such is he adored by the Templar.

"And when they were come unto a place called Golgotha, that is to say, a place of a skull." Matt. xxvii: 33.

Golgotha literally means "a heap of skulls," but three of the Evangelists define it as "a place of a skull." Luke says, "which is called Calvary," that is, "a skull." The Greek word is ... which the Vulgate renders *Calvariam*, meaning "a bare skull." It is probable the name was given this elevation because of its peculiarly shaped summit.

The awful tragedy enacted on Golgotha is dear to the true Templar, and he ever holds his sword in readiness to defend the religion founded upon that tragedy.

Moreover the Lord said unto me, Take thee a great roll, and write in it with a man's pen concerning Maher-shalal-hash-baz." Isaiah viii: i.

An attempt at literal rendering of this passage would result in, "Take thee a great roll, and write in it with a man's pen concerning Make speed to the spoil, hasten the prey." The phrase is as difficult of translation as is the phrase, "Anathema Maran-atha." It means in its naked form, "Hasten-booty, Speed- spoil." It is pronounced *Mā-her shălăl hăsh ´băz.*

This phrase was cherished by the ancient Templars, who held it to be symbolical of that readiness for action which should characterize a true Soldier of Christ!

"At the same time came to them Tatnai, governor on this side the river, and Shethar-boznai, and their companions, and said thus unto them, Who hath commanded you to build this house and to make up this wall? " Ezra v: 3.

This Tat na-i was Satrap of the province west of the Euphrates, next to Judea. Shethar-boz na-i was not a Satrap, but an officer of rank, and though his name meant "star of splendor," he united with Tatnai in an effort to shroud with gloom the hopes of the returned children of the captivity. God caused their wrath to praise him.

THE SO-CALLED VISION
OF CONSTANTINE.

A fable invented by the sycophants of Constantine has been dignified into a Motto of the valiant and magnanimous Order of the Temple, after passing through various gradations of fortune. The fable is thus related:

Constantine the Great was declared Augustus and Pontifex Maximus after he had vanquished the army of Marentius, under the walls of Rome. He professed Christianity. It was during his march on . Rome, and while encamped near Mentz, that he was reported to have seen in the sky a fiery Cross, bearing the inscription Ἐ ῳ

"With this sign you will conquer." He had this symbol, known as the Cross of Constantine, emblazoned on the Imperial Standard, called the *Labarum*.

How the *Chi Rho* Cross came to be changed into the Passion Cross of the Latin Church, and the Greek inscription into corresponding Latin, is clearly explained by the conquest of the Eastern by the Western Church. When the Church of Rome became mistress of the world everything had to submit to its dictation, and all popular myths gravitated to its use and emolument.

It is deeply to be regretted that the name of Constantine, who murdered his father-in-law, his brother- in-law, his nephew, his son, and finally his wife, Fausta, should be associated with this popular myth, and this beautiful symbol. That he was ever converted to Christianity we deny, and his being baptized only in the year in which he died, nearly a quarter of a century after his professed conversion, proves his deception.

It is not established that the ancient Templars used either the Greek or the Latin inscription so popular with the modern Templars.

They did use the Passion Cross on the Beauceant, and as a part of their armorial bearings.

AN HISTORICAL FACT.

Simon of Syracuse, a Templar, betrayed his trust to the Saracens. Saladin, despising this Templar's treason, had his head struck off and sent it to the Grand Master of the Templars, who ordered it placed on the top of the longest spear in camp, as a warning to all traitors.

The Canadians relate that the head was "placed on a pole, or spire." The Scotch say, "on the point of a spear or pike." The head of one so despicable, if to be elevated at all, should be "placed upon the highest spire of Christendom," as a warning to all traitors.

DRESS OF THE ANCIENT TEMPLARS.

The ancient Templars habitually wore a long, white Tunic, or Cassock, cut like that of the priests, with a red Cross before and behind. The Girdle was worn over the Shirt and under the Tunic. The serving brethren wore dark Kirtles to distinguish them from the Knights, all being clad in white. The white Mantle, with its red Cross on the left breast, and a Hood, was worn over all. The material was always light, because of the great heat of Palestine.

In 1162 the Pope permitted the Templars to receive into their houses spiritual persons, not bound by any previous vow. After one year's novitiate these were initiated, as were the lay Knights. The habit of the Chaplain was a white Tunic and red Cross: but none under a Bishop could wear a white Mantle.

The Chaplain wore the baret, or Cap.

There is a dispute as to the form of the Red Cross of the Order. We favor the form given elsewhere, on the *Vexillum Belli*, as the one used by the ancient Templars, though some say the Cross on the left breast of the white Mantle was of "four arms, the under one being the longest."

The arms of a Knight Templar were a Sword, Lance, Mace and Shield, and his head was covered by the Hood attached to his Mantle. He was allowed three horses and an esquire, who was a serving brother; or a hireling, who was a layman.

THE ANCIENT MOTTO.

The Grand Encampment has adopted this reading of the Motto of the ancient Templars:

"*Non nobis Domine; non nobis, sed Nomini tuo da gloriam.*"

In the "Biblia Sacra," published in Antwerp in 1605, we find this reading of it:

"*Non nobis Domine, non nobis: sed Nomini tuo da gloriam.*"

These words are found in the "*Biblia Sacra*" as part of Psalm cxiii, verse 31. In the Accepted Version they form part of Psalm cxv: 1. It is probable that the omission of the comma after the second *nobis*, page 79, St. Louis Ritual, was a typographical blunder. As that Ritual no longer exists, the official reading adopted for the Grand Standard remains in force.

"IT IS FINISHED."

In its Latin form,—"*Consummatum est*,"—this was a cherished phrase of the ancient Templar usage. It is to be regretted that its use appears to be entirely dropped by the Modern Order in the United States.

Would it not be a proper complement of the phrase, "*In hoc Signo Vinces*," and on reversing the position to use "*Consummatum est*"?

CEREMONIAL OBSERVANCES OF THE ORDER.

DEDICATION AND CONSECRATION OF ASYLUMS.

THE Triangle has twelve Tapers properly displayed upon it. No other equipments thereon.

The Commandery is opened, and the Grand Commander and Staff received according to the Tactics of the Jurisdiction.

EC.—Right Eminent Grand Commander, the members of — Commandery, No. —, animated by zeal for the Order and veneration for the ceremonies thereof, have prepared and furnished this Asylum, and now crave that you dedicate and consecrate the same to the solemn rites of the Order of the Temple.

GC.—Eminent Sir, I congratulate — Commandery on the appearance of the Asylum which their liberality and good taste have prepared for the observance of the ceremonies of the Order. It receives our entire approbation, and at your request we will proceed to Consecrate the same to the solemn uses for which it is intended.

GCG.—Sir Knights, ATTENTION! UNCOVER!

GC.—Excellent Grand Prelate, lead us in the Prayer of Dedication.

ALMIGHTY and Most Merciful Father, look upon us, Thy children, bowed in Thy presence, and graciously accept the service in which we are engaged. May the meetings to be held in this Asylum be under Thy protection and guidance, and may all its members be of one mind to honor and obey Thee, and love and protect one another. And may the work done in this Asylum receive Thy approval and benediction.

And to thy great and holy Name shall be all the praise and glory, through Jesus Christ our Saviour, AMEN.

GCG.—Sir Knights, RE-COVER!

GC.—Sir Knights, BE SEATED! Give reverent heed to the ceremony of Consecration, to the end that all may be endued with a proper appreciation of the uses to which this Asylum is about to be set apart.

Excellent Grand Prelate, place upon the Triangle the Holy Bible, opened at the third chapter of the Gospel by John.

Prelate places open Bible in center of Triangle.

GC. (Rising and uncovering)—To God the Father, who so loved the world as to give His Son to be the Captain of our Salvation, I dedicate this Asylum. May Peace be within its walls. (*Recovers.*)

GC.—Sir Knight Grand Generalissimo, place upon the Holy Bible an emblem of Mortality.

Grand Generalissimo places a skull upon the Bible.

GC. (*Uncovering*)—To Him who hath abolished death, and hath brought life and immortality to light through the Gospel, I

Dedicate this Asylum. May the unity of that Faith be maintained in this place. (*Re-covers.*)

GC.–Sir Knight Grand Captain General, light the Tapers.

The Grand Captain General lights the Tapers on the Triangle.

GC.–To the memory of Hugh de Payen, the founder of the Order of the Temple, I set this Asylum apart to the solemn uses of that Order. Sir Knights, may brotherly love prevail, and every moral and social virtue cement you.

MUSIC.

"Nearer, My God, to Thee," or some other appropriate Hymn, will be sung.

GC.–Sir Knights, this Asylum thus solemnly set apart to the ceremonies of our Order must not be profaned by improper assemblies, nor desecrated by observances not in accord with the spirit of Christian Knighthood. Guard well its doors from improper invasions, and allow none to enter but such as are duly qualified when the trumpet of the Sentinel has sounded the Assembly.

Here meet in the fear of God, and with the spirit of true and chivalrous Knights. Be true to each other and to yourselves. Pray for the prosperity of the Order, and diligently labor for the peace of the Commandery of which you are members. You will arise and uncover.

We will now unite with our Excellent Grand Prelate in:

PRAYER.

MERCIFUL Father, we again thank Thee for the pleasures of this sacred hour. Consecrate with Thy Benediction this Asylum which Thy servant has so solemnly dedicated to Thee, so that all things done herein may be prospered by Thy goodness and approved by Thy wisdom.

Bless our beloved Order, wherever dispersed, and when the end shall come, as come it will, may we all be received into that Rest which remaineth to the people of God. Through Jesus Christ our Redeemer, AMEN.

BENEDICTION.

Grace be with you, mercy, and peace, from God the Father, and from the Lord Jesus Christ, the Son of the Father, in truth and love.

GC.—Sir Knights, RE-COVER! BE SEATED!

CONSTITUTING NEW COMMANDERIES.

THE Knights about to be constituted into a Commandery will assemble in the Asylum on the appointed day, and open a Commandery of Knights Templar. The Triangle should be fully equipped, but the Tapers to be unlighted. The Jewels are placed upon a small Table or Altar, in the West, and covered with a white cloth.

The Commandery opened, the Grand Officers will be received according to the Tactics of the Jurisdiction. When the Grand Officers are in their stations, then—

G. MAR.–Right Eminent Grand Commander, a constitutional number of Knights of the Valiant and Magnanimous Order of the Temple, duly instructed in the sublime mysteries of our Order, having received from the proper authority a Warrant or Charter, authorizing them to hold a regular Commandery of Knights Templar, are now assembled for the purpose of being legally constituted, and having their Officers installed, in due and ancient form.

GC.–Let the Constituting ceremonies begin. The Choir will render appropriate Music.

The Choir will sing appropriate Music, as chosen.

GC.—Excellent Grand Prelate, read unto us a Lesson.

Grand Prelate reads Psalm lxiii: 1-8.

GC.—Excellent Grand Prelate, lead us in Prayer. GCG.—Commandery, ATTENTION! UNCOVER!

PRAYER.

ALMIGHTY God, our Heavenly Father, with whom is life, and from whom cometh every good and perfect gift, unto Thee do we bow our hearts in reverence and in trust, gratefully acknowledging Thy mercies and the manifold manifestations of Thy providence and Thy love. And now, as we engage in the solemn services of this occasion, we beseech Thy guidance and direction, that all things may be done to Thy glory and to the advancement of the interests we have in charge. Let Thy grace be upon these Thy servants about to be constituted into an organization founded upon the Christian religion and the practice of the Christian virtues. Give unto them a large appreciation of the mission to which they are called, and an earnest purpose to perform the duties which will henceforth devolve upon them.

Enlighten their minds, purify their hearts, and help them to attain that true consecration of soul, which will enable them to bear much fruit to the honor and glory of Thy holy Name.

All this we ask, most Merciful Father, through him who is the Resurrection and the Life, our Lord and Saviour, Jesus Christ. AMEN.

LORD'S PRAYER follows (in which all unite).

GCG.–Sir Knights, RE-COVER! GC.–Sir Knights, BE SEAT-
ED!

MUSIC.

GC.–Sir Knight Recorder, read aloud the Charter issued to
this Commandery.

Recorder reads the Charter aloud.

GC.–   ♪♪♪ Sir Knights, do you still approve the Officers
named in this Charter, and desire their installation?

If the Knights shall answer–"We do,"–then–

GCG.–Sir Knights, *Draw* SWORDS! *Present* SWORDS!

GC.–By virtue of the high power and authority in me vested, I
do now form you, Sir Knights, into a just and regular Commandery of Knights Templar. Henceforth you are authorized
and empowered to form and open a Council of Knights of the
Red Cross, a Commandery of Knights Templar and Knights of
Malta, of the Order of St. John of Jerusalem, and to perform all
such things as may appertain to the same; conforming in all your
doings to the Laws and Constitution of the Grand Commandery
under whose authority you act, and to the Constitution and
Edicts of the Grand Encampment of the United States. And may
the God of our fathers be with you, guide and direct you in all
your undertakings.

*The Jewels are now uncovered by the Grand Wardens; sol-
emn Music.*

131

GC.–Excellent Grand Prelate, you will now pronounce the words of CONSECRATION.

GP.–To our Most Eminent and Worthy Patron, St. John the Almoner, I do now solemnly dedicate this – Commandery, by the name and title of Commandery; and may the God of all grace abundantly bless it and all its members in their laudable undertakings; and may each one of its members so redeem his time, that he may receive the joyful invitation, "Enter thou into the joy of thy Lord."

GP.–Glory to God in the highest, and on earth peace, good will toward men.

THE KNIGHTS.–AS it was in the beginning, is now, and ever shall be, world without end. AMEN.

GCG.–Sir Knights, Carry SWORDS!

The Grand Wardens now light the Tapers on the Triangle.

MUSIC.

The "DOXOLOGY" (in which all will unite).

GP.–The Lord bless thee, and keep thee: the Lord make his face shine upon thee, and be gracious unto thee: the Lord lift up his countenance upon thee, and give thee peace.
THE KNIGHTS.–AMEN! AMEN! AMEN!

GC.–Sir Knight Grand Marshal, make Proclamation in the East.

G. MAR.–Hear ye! Valiant Knights of the Temple!

I am ordered to proclaim that this new Commandery of Knights Templar and the Appendant Orders, by the name of – Commandery, has been legally constituted according to the forms and ceremonies of the Order of Knights Templar; and it is now authorized to meet and work as a regular Commandery under the jurisdiction of the Grand Commandery of —.

GCG.—Sir Knights, *Return* SWORDS! GC.—Sir Knights, BE SEATED!

INSTALLATION OF OFFICERS
OF A COMMANDERY.

THE Commandery having been duly constituted, the Officers are to be installed with the following ceremony: The Table, on which lie the Jewels, is placed in front of the Grand Commander, and the Tapers on the Triangle are lighted.

The Commandery is opened, and the Grand Commander, and his Staff, are received according to the Tactics of the Jurisdiction.

The Officers to be installed having withdrawn to another room, the ceremonies will begin thus:

GC.—Let the Officers you have chosen, and desire to have installed at this time, enter.

The Grand Marshal conducts the Officers elect into the Asylum. The Grand Commander will cause the Commandery to arise. The Officers elect will he escorted to the East in single file, and so arranged that when their left flank faces the East the Officers will be standing thus:

W. SwB. StB. Rec. Tr. JW. SW. P. CG. G. EC.

The Officers will enter with Swords at Carry, and when they have reached the East the Marshal will command—

MAR.—*File* RIGHT! (*When in proper place*) HALT! *Left* FACE! *Present* SWORDS!

MAR. (*Saluting*)—Right Eminent Grand Commander, these are the Officers chosen by this Commandery, whose installation is desired at this time.

GC.—Sir Knights, *Carry* SWORDS! *Return* SWORDS! BE SEATED!

All obey these commands, and the Officers are seated on chairs previously located for them.

GC.—Sir Knight Marshal, present the Eminent Commander for installation.

Marshal lakes the Commander by left arm and conducts him to the Altar, which had been placed, with the Jewels thereon, in front of the GC.

MAR.—Right Eminent Grand Commander, I have the honor to present to you Eminent Sir —, who has been elected to the office of Commander of this Commandery. I find him to be well skilled in our sublime mysteries, and observant of the noble precepts of our forefathers, and therefore I have no doubt but that he will discharge the important duties of his office with fidelity.

GC.—Eminent Sir, are you ready to subscribe to the Vow of office?

If the Commander elect answers that he is, then the Grand Commander will draw his Sword, and hold it horizontally, the edge toward the Commander elect, who will grasp the blade with his left hand, and place his right hand on his left breast.

GC.—You will repeat after me—

I, – –, do promise and vow that I will support and maintain the Constitution and Code of Statutes of the Grand Encampment of Knights Templar of the United States of America; that I will support and maintain the Bylaws of this Commandery, and the Laws, Constitution, Rules and Edicts of the Grand Commandery under whose immediate authority I act; and I will, to the best of my knowledge and ability, faithfully discharge the various duties incumbent upon the office to which I have been elected.

GC.–Eminent Sir, having been elected to the important and honorable station of Commander of this Commandery, it is with unfeigned pleasure that I enter upon the discharge of the duty of installing you into office. As the head of a Christian institution you are charged with important responsibilities and duties, and it is confidently anticipated that your fidelity to these trusts will reflect honor upon yourself and credit upon your Commandery. It now becomes my duty to propose certain questions to you, to which unequivocal answers are required: Do you solemnly promise, upon the honor of a Knight Templar—

I. That you will redouble your endeavors to correct the vices, purify the morals, and promote the happiness of those of your brethren who have attained this magnanimous Order?

II. That you will never suffer your Commandery to be opened, unless there be present nine regular Knights of the Order?

III. That you will not confer the Orders upon anyone who has not shown a charitable disposition, or who has not made a considerable proficiency in the foregoing degrees.

IV. That you will promote the general good of our Order, and on all proper occasions be ready to give and receive instructions, and particularly from the General and State Grand Officers?

V. That, to the utmost of your power, you will preserve the solemnities of our ceremonies, and behave, in open Commandery, with the most profound respect and reverence, as an example to your brethren?

VI. That you will not acknowledge or have intercourse with any Commandery that does not work under a constitutional warrant or dispensation?

VII. That you will not admit any visitor into your Commandery who has not been knighted in a Commandery legally constituted, without his first being formally healed?

VIII. That you will pay due respect and obedience to the instructions of the General and State Grand Officers, particularly relating to the several Lectures and Charges, and will resign the chair to them, severally, when they may visit your Commandery?

IX. That you will support and observe the Constitution of the Grand Encampment of the United States, and the Statutes and Regulations of the Grand Commandery under whose authority you act?

X. That you will bind your successor in office to the observance of the same rules to which you have now assented?

Do you submit to all these things, and do you promise to observe and practice them faithfully?

The Eminent Commander assents. Grand Commander returns his Sword.

GC.–Eminent Commander, having been chosen by the Knights of your Commandery to fill the most exalted station in their power to bestow, I congratulate you upon being the recipient of such honorable preferment, and now invest you with the Jewel of your office, which is a Cross surrounded by rays of light. It is to remind you that *humility, love,* and pure *benevolence* are refulgent rays that emanate from the pure and undefiled religion of the blessed Emmanuel, and which should ever characterize the members of this Christian Order. It is to remind you of Him who died that He might give life to the world, and who is indeed the Lord and Saviour of all those who accept His guidance and obey His precepts.

I present you the Charter of your Commandery.

You will receive it as a sacred deposit, and never permit it to be used for any other purposes than those expressed in it, and safely transmit it to your successor in office.

I also commit to your hands the Holy Bible, the great light in every degree of Masonry. The doctrines contained in this sacred volume create in us a belief in the existence of the Eternal Jehovah, the only true and living God, the Creator and Judge of all things in heaven and on earth; they also confirm in us a belief in the dispensations of His providence. This belief strengthens our Faith, and enables us to ascend the first step of the Grand Masonic ladder. This Faith naturally produces in us a Hope of becoming partakers in the promises expressed in this inestimable gift of God to man, which Hope enables us to ascend the second step; but the third and last, being Charity, comprehends the former, and will continue to exert its influence when Faith shall be lost in sight, and Hope in complete fruition. The Cross

Swords, testing upon the Holy Bible, are to remind us that we should he "strong in the Lord, and in the power of His might;" that we should put on the whole armour of God, to be able to wrestle successfully against principalities and powers, and spiritual wickedness in high places.

I also present you the Constitution of the Grand Encampment of the United States of America, the Rules and Regulations of the Grand Commandery of this State, and the By-laws of your Commandery. You will frequently consult them yourself, and cause them to be read for the information of your Commandery, that all, being informed of their duty, may have no reasonable excuse to offer for the neglect of it.

And now, Eminent Sir, permit me to induct you into the chair of your Commandery, and in behalf of the Knights here assembled, to offer you my most sincere congratulations on your accession to the honorable station you now fill. It will henceforth be your special duty to preserve inviolate the Constitution and Laws of the Order; to dispense justice, reward merit, inculcate the almighty force and the importance of truth, and diffuse the sublime principles of universal benevolence. You will distribute alms to poor and weary pilgrims traveling from afar, feed the hungry, clothe the naked, and bind up the wounds of the afflicted. You will inculcate the duties of charity and hospitality, and govern your Commandery with justice and moderation. And finally, my brother, may the bright example of the illustrious heroes of former ages, whose matchless valor has shed undying lustre on the name of Knight Templar, encourage and animate you to the faithful performance of every duty.

GCG.—Commandery, ATTENTION! *Draw* SWORDS! *Present* SWORDS!

GC.—Sir Knights, Behold your Eminent Commander! Recollect that the prosperity of your Commandery will as much depend on your support, assistance and obedience, as on the assiduity, fidelity and wisdom of your Commander.

Be ye therefore diligent and faithful in the performance of your respective duties.

The new Commander having made any remarks he desired—

GCG.—Carry SWORDS! Return SWORDS! GC.—Sir Knights, BE SEATED!

GC.—Prepare the remaining Officers for installation. MAR.—Officers elect, ATTENTION! Prepare for taking the Vow!

The Marshal will cause the odd numbers to draw their Swords. and drop them to the left, in front of the breasts of the even numbers. The even numbers will grasp the blades of these Swords with their right hands. When all is ready—

MAR.—Officers elect, UNCOVER!

MAR.—Right Eminent Grand Commander, the Officers elect are in proper position to take upon themselves the Vow of office.

GC.—Before proceeding to install you into your respective stations it is my duty to administer to each of you the Vow of office. Do you severally consent to take upon yourselves that Vow?

Each must assent for himself.

GC.—Then repeat after me:

I, — —, do promise and vow that I will maintain and support the Constitution and Code of Statutes of the Grand Encampment of the United States of America, the Constitution, Rules and Edicts of the Grand Commandery of – –, and that I will, to the best of my ability, faithfully discharge the duties of the office to which I have been elected.

MAR.–Officers elect, RE-COVER! *Carry* SWORDS!

GC.–Sir Knights, BE SEATED! Sir Knight Marshal, present the Generalissimo.

MAR.–Right Eminent Grand Commander, I present Sir – –, who has been chosen Generalissimo of this Commandery, for installation.

CHARGE TO THE GENERALISSIMO.

GC.–Sir, you have been elected Generalissimo of this Commandery. I now invest you with the Jewel of your office, which is a Square, surmounted by a Paschal Lamb. When beholding the Lamb, let it stimulate you to have, at all times, a watchful eye over your own conduct, and an earnest solicitude for the prosperity of the kingdom of the blessed Emmanuel, the spotless Lamb of God, who was slain from the foundation of the world.

The Square is to remind you that the same principles of brotherly love and friendship should forever govern the members of Freemasonry and of the Orders of Knighthood. Your station is on the right of your Commander; your duty is to assist him in his various duties, and, in his absence, to preside. I charge you, therefore, to be faithful to the Sir Knights with whom you are associated; put them often in remembrance of those things which tend to their everlasting peace. Finally, "preach the word; be instant in season, out of season; reprove, rebuke, exhort with all longsuffering and doctrine;" ever remembering the promise, "Be thou faithful unto death, and I will give thee a crown of life."

CHARGE TO THE CAPTAIN GENERAL.

Sir, you are elected Captain General of this Commandery. I now invest you with the Jewel of your office, which is a Level, surmounted by a Cock. As the undaunted courage and valor of the Cock stimulates him to conquer his competitor, or yield himself a victim to the contest, so should you be stimulated to the discharge of every duty. You should have on "the breastplate of righteousness," so that with patience and meekness you may ever travel on the *level* of humility, and be so supplied with divine grace as to prevent you from selling your God or denying your Master. Your station is on the left of your Commander. Your duty, among other things, is to see that due preparation is made for the various meetings of the Commandery; that the Chambers and Asylum are in suitable array for the introduction of candidates and the dispatch of business. You are also to receive and communicate to the lines all orders issued by the Eminent Commander. You are to assist in Council, and, in the absence of your Commander and Generalissimo, you are to preside over the Commandery. And now, I exhort you, that with fidelity you perform every duty; and whatsoever ye do, do *it* heartily, as to the Lord, and not unto men; continue in prayer, and watch in the same with thanksgiving; ever bearing in mind the promise, "Be not weary in well doing: for in due season we shall reap, if we faint not."

CHARGE TO THE PRELATE.

Sir, you are elected Prelate of this Commandery. I have the pleasure of investing you with this Triple Triangle, which is the Jewel of your office, and a beautiful emblem of Jehovah. Your station is on the right of the Generalissimo; your duty is to officiate at the Altar and to offer up prayers to Deity. Your Jewel is to remind you of the importance of the trust reposed in you. And may He who is able, abundantly furnish you for every good work, preserve you from falling into error, improve, strengthen, establish and perfect you; and finally greet you with, "Well done, thou good and faithful servant: enter thou into the joy of thy Lord."

CHARGE TO THE SENIOR WARDEN.

Sir, you are elected Senior Warden of this Commandery. I now invest you with the Jewel of your office, which is a Hollow Square and Sword of Justice. It is to remind you that, as the children of Israel marched in a hollow square in their journey through the wilderness, in order to guard and protect the Ark of the Covenant, so should you be vigilant in guarding every avenue from innovation and error.

Let the Sword, therefore, be ever drawn to guard the Constitution of the Order. Your station is at the Southwest angle of the Triangle, and upon the right of the First Division. You will attend Pilgrim Warriors, comfort and support Pilgrim Penitents, and after due trial, introduce them into the Asylum. Let it be your constant care that the warrior be not deterred from duty, nor the penitent molested on his journey. Finally, let your light so shine before men, that they may see your good works, and glorify your Father which is in heaven.

CHARGE TO THE JUNIOR WARDEN.

Sir, you are elected Junior Warden of this Commandery. I now invest you with the Jewel of your office, which is an Eagle and Flaming Sword. It is to remind you to perform your various duties with justice and valor, having an eagle eye on the prosperity of the Order. Your station is at the Northwest angle of the Triangle. Your duty is to attend poor and weary pilgrims traveling from afar, accompany them on their journey, and in due time recommend them to the Eminent Commander. You will be careful that, in addition to the pilgrim's garb, sandals, staff and scrip, their whole preparation and deportment shall be such as to cause them to be recognized as children of humility. Teach them that "*Magna est Veritas, et Prævalebit,*" is the Motto of the Order; and although they will often find the heights of fortune inaccessible, and the thorny path of life crooked, adverse and forlorn, yet, by faith and humility—courage, constancy, patience and perseverance—they may gain admission into the Asylum above; there to enjoy the rewards that await the valiant soldiers of the Lord Jesus Christ.

Finally, be ye perfect, always abounding in the work of the Lord, that you may be a shining light in the world. A city that is set on a hill can not be hid.

CHARGE TO THE TREASURER.

Sir, you are elected Treasurer of this Commandery. I now invest you with the Jewel of your office. Your station is on the right of the Generalissimo, in front. The qualities which should recommend a Treasurer are accuracy and fidelity; accuracy, in keeping a fair and minute account of all receipts and disbursements; fidelity, in carefully preserving all the property and funds of the Commandery that may be placed in his hands, and rendering a just account of the same whenever he is called upon for that purpose. I presume that your respect and attachment to the Commandery, and. your earnest solicitude for a good name, which is better than precious ointment, will prompt you to the faithful discharge of the duties of your office.

CHARGE TO THE RECORDER.

Sir, you are elected Recorder of this Commandery. I now invest you with the Jewel of your office. Your station is on the left of the Captain General, in front. The qualities which should recommend a Recorder are, promptitude in issuing the notifications and orders of his superior officers, punctuality in attending the meetings of the Commandery, correctness in recording their proceedings, judgment in discriminating between what is proper and what is improper to be committed to writing, integrity in accounting for all moneys that may pass through his hands, and fidelity in paying the same over into the hands of the Treasurer. The possession of these good qualities, I presume, has designated you for this important office, and I can not entertain a doubt that you will discharge its duties beneficially to the Commandery and honorably to yourself. And when you shall have completed the record of Your transactions here below, and finished the term of your probation, may you be admitted into the celestial Asylum of saints and angels, and find your name recorded in the Lamb's Book of Life.

CHARGE TO THE STANDARD BEARER.

Sir, you are elected Standard Bearer of this Commandery. I now invest you with the Jewel of your office, which is a Plumb, surmounted by a Banner. Your station is in the West, and in the center of the Second Division. Your duty is to display, support and protect the Standard of our Order, which I now, with pleasure, confide to your valor. You will remember that it is our rallying point in time of danger; and when unfurled in a just and virtuous cause, you will never relinquish it to an enemy but with your life. Let, therefore, your conduct be such as all the virtuous will delight to imitate; let the refulgent rays which ever emanate from pure benevolence and humility, diffuse their lustre on all around, that it may encourage and animate all true and courteous Knights, and, at the same time, confound and dismay all their enemies.

CHARGE TO THE SWORD BEARER.

Sir, you are elected Sword Bearer of this Commandery. I now invest you with the Jewel of your office, which is a Triangle and Cross Swords. Your station is on the right of the Standard Bearer, and on the right of the Second Division when separately formed. Your duty is to assist in protecting the Banners of our Order, with a heart devoted to the principles of Faith, Hope and

Charity. Holding the mystic sword that is-endowed with justice and fortitude, and tempered with mercy, you may cast your eyes upon the Standard, and recall that "*In Hoc Signo Vinces*" is not only an expressive Motto of our Order, but is consoling to the heart of every believer.

CHARGE TO THE WARDER.

Sir, you are elected Warder of this Commandery. I now invest you with the Jewel of your office, which is a Square Plate, with a Trumpet and Cross Swords engraved thereon. Your station is upon the left of the Standard Bearer, and upon the left of the Second Division, when formed in line. Your duty is to sound the Assembly, announce the approach and departure of the Eminent Commander, to post the Sentinels, and see that the Asylum is duly guarded. You will, also, report all petitions from visitors and strangers. I charge you to be punctual in your attendance, and indefatigable in the discharge of your important duties; for, though yours is among the last offices in the Commandery, it is by no means the least in importance.

CHARGE TO THE SENTINEL.

Sir Knight, you are appointed Sentinel. I now invest you with the Jewel of your office, which is a Square Plate, with a Battle Axe engraved thereon. Your post is that of honor as well as of danger. You will, therefore, be vigilant, challenge with spirit, examine with caution, admonish with candor, relieve cheerfully, protect with fidelity, and fight valiantly.

GCG.–Commandery, ATTENTION! *Draw* SWORDS!

CHARGE TO THE COMMANDERY.

Sir Knights, to manage and conduct the concerns of a Commandery of Knights Templar with that promptitude, integrity and skill which the institution demands, will require the exercise of all the talents and perseverance of its Officers and members. Are any of you solicitous that your equals and inferiors should conduct themselves toward you with deference and respect? you will be sure to let no opportunity pass without furnishing them an example in your own conduct. The Officers will recollect that those moral and religious duties and precepts which they, from time to time, so forcibly impress upon the minds of others, should by no means be neglected by themselves; and the most effectual way to insure success is to let precept and example go hand in hand.

I would therefore exhort you to look well to the East, to the West, to the North, and to the South, and see that the entering avenues are strictly guarded, and that you suffer no one to pass the threshold of your Asylum but the worthy children of humility; and, at the same time, that you suffer no one to walk among you disorderly without admonition or reproof. While such is the conduct of the Officers and members, you may rest assured that this valiant, magnanimous Order will forever flourish like the green bay tree.

And now, Sir Knights, I would address you in the language of David to his beloved city, Peace be within thy walls, *and* prosperity within thy palaces. For my brethren and companions' sakes, I will now say, Peace *be* within thee.

The Marshal then proclaims the [new] Commandery in the following manner, viz.:

In the name of the Grand Commandery of the State of —, I proclaim this Commandery , by the name of — Commandery, No.—, to be legally constituted, consecrated, and the Officers duly installed.

After the necessary business is finished, the Commandery is closed.

GRAND COMMANDERIES.

INSTALLATION OF THEIR OFFICERS.

THE Grand Commander will appoint a Grand Marshal, under whose direction the Officers elect will retire to an adjoining room. The Jewels will be placed on a table, which is in front of the Installing Officer. The Altar is beside this table. Twelve chairs will be placed just west of the Altar, as seats for the Officers elect when they enter. The chairs will extend from North to South, the seat of the Grand Commander on the right, and of the Grand Warder on the left.

GC.—Let the Grand Officers elect enter.

The Grand Marshal, who is notified by the Captain of the Guard, conducts the Officers elect, in single file, to the East, and halts them in front of the chairs, facing the East.

GC. (*As Officers enter*)— ♪ ♪ ♪

If there is an instrument, a March will be played.

G. Mar. (*When the Officers are halted, facing East*)—Right Eminent Commander, these are the Officers chosen by the Grand Commandery, and they are now ready for installation.

GC.—Excellent Grand Prelate, lead us in an Invocation to the Throne of Grace. Sir Knights, Attention! Uncover!

The Grand Prelate offers the following, or some other:

PRAYER.

Almighty God, our Heavenly Father, from whom cometh every good and perfect gift, we humbly approach Thy presence, and beseech Thee, for the sake of Thine only begotten Son, to look upon us in infinite mercy, and bless this our Commander, and those associated with him in office, with a rich outpouring of Thy grace. Pardon our sins, and blot out our transgressions from before Thee! Incline the hearts of these Officers to follow after Thee! Endow them with wisdom, and give unto each patience, perseverance, courage, constancy, faith, and humility.

Lord's Prayer (in which all unite).

GC.—Sir Knights, Re-cover!

GC.—Sir Knights, before investing you with the Jewels of your official positions, it becomes my duty to receive from you the Vow of office. Are you willing to take such a Vow?

The Grand Commander and all the Officers elect bow in assent.

GC.—Let the Grand Commander elect approach the East.

The Grand Marshal conducts him to the East.

GC. (*GC. draws his Sword and holds it vertically*)—You will grasp the blade of this Sword with your left hand, and then place your right hand upon your heart. (*Done.*) Now repeat after me:

VOW OF OFFICE.

I, —, do solemnly promise and vow, that I will maintain and support the Constitution of the Grand Encampment of Knights Templar of the United States of America, the Statutes and Regulations of the Grand Commandery of the State of — and that I will, to the best of my ability, faithfully discharge the duties of the office to which I have been elected.

Installing Officer returns his Sword to scabbard.

CHARGE.

GC.—Right Eminent Sir, having been called by the members of this Grand Body to fill the highest office in their gift, I congratulate you upon having received such distinction at their hands, and I now invest you with the Jewel of your office.

Your authority will at all times be respected and your orders will be cheerfully obeyed. It is expected that you will not only have a watchful care over the interests of the Order in your jurisdiction, and enforce a prompt obedience to its Rules and Regulations, but that you will yourself exemplify, in your daily walk and conversation, the excellent tenets of your profession; that your ears will never be closed to the cry of the widow and the orphan; and that you will not turn aside from injured innocence, or from a frater in distress. Maintain with unfaltering zeal the Statutes and Regulations of this Grand Body, and by your own respect for law prompt others to a cheerful obedience of all lawful requirements. You will now assume your station.

The Grand Commander is escorted by the Grand Marshal to his station, where he stands.

GC.–Sir Knights, *Present* SWORDS! Behold your Grand Commander! Grand Commander, behold the Grand Commandery!

Remarks by the new Grand Commander will now be in order. He will install the remaining Officers, or may request the Installing Officer to continue.

GC.–Sir Knights, *Carry* SWORDS! *Return* Swords BE SEATED!

GC.–Remaining Officers elect (*they arise*): Before proceeding to invest you with the honors and responsibilities of your several offices, it becomes my duty to administer to you the Obligation of office. As you have severally consented to take upon yourselves that Obligation, place yourselves in position to take that Vow.

The Grand Marshal will then cause each Sir Knight in the line of Officers elect occupying the odd number from the right of the line, to draw his Sword, and drop it to the left to a horizontal position. The Sir Knight on his left will lay his left hand upon the Sword, then each places his right hand upon his left breast, and repeats after the Grand Commander the following Vow:

GC.–Repeat after me:

I, –, do solemnly promise and vow, that I will maintain and support the Constitution, Laws, and Statutes of the Grand Encampment of the United States, the Constitution, Statutes, and Regulations of this Grand Commandery, and that I will, to the best of my ability, discharge the duties of the office to which I have been chosen.

GC.–Escort the Deputy Grand Commander to the East, and the remainder of the Officers elect will resume their seats.

G. MAR.–Right Eminent Grand Commander, I present unto you Very Eminent Sir –, who has been elected Deputy Grand Commander of this Grand Commandery, and who is now ready for installation.

GC.–In the exalted station to which you have been chosen, Very Eminent Sir, you are the immediate representative of the Grand Commander, and in case of unforeseen casualty to him—which God forbid—you are to enter upon his functions and assume his responsibilities. The elevated position you are thus called to occupy demands a corresponding zeal and devotion on your part, which, I doubt not, you will ever be found ready to exercise. I now invest you with the Jewel of your office, and will only remind you that you are henceforward on duty, and that the faithful soldier and valiant Knight sleeps not at his post.

The Grand Marshal will present the remaining Officers in the same manner, when the Installing Officer will deliver to them the following Charges:

CHARGE TO THE GRAND GENERALISSIMO.

Eminent Sir, having been elected to the important station of Grand Generalissimo, I take great pleasure in investing you with the appropriate Jewel of your office. Your station is on the right of the Grand Commander, and the exercise of all your talents and zeal will be necessary in the discharge of your various duties.

In the absence of your superior officers, the command will devolve upon you. I charge you, therefore, to be faithful to your associates; put them often in remembrance of those things which tend to their everlasting peace; be instant in season, out of season; reprove, rebuke, exhort with all longsuffering and doctrine, ever remembering the promise, "Be thou faithful unto death, and I will give thee a crown of life."

CHARGE TO THE GRAND CAPTAIN GENERAL.

Eminent Sir, the office of Grand Captain General, to which you have been elected, is one of the most important in the gift of the Grand Commandery, and I now invest you with the Jewel of your office. Your station is on the left of the Grand Commander, and you are to assist him and your associate officers in council, and in their absence to govern the Grand Commandery. You are to have in charge the Grand Asylum, and see that it is in suitable array for the dispatch of business. Improve your opportunities in extending knightly courtesy and hospitality to all true and faithful Sir Knights, and in the preservation of harmony within the bounds of our jurisdiction; and whatsoever ye do, do *it* heartily, as to the Lord, and not unto men; continue in prayer, and watch in the same with thanksgiving; ever bearing in mind the promise, "Be not weary in well doing: for in due season we shall reap, if we faint not."

CHARGE TO THE GRAND PRELATE.

Revered Sir, to you has been assigned the sacred duties of the office of Grand Prelate, and I invest you with the appropriate

Jewel of your office. Your station will be on the right of the Grand Generalissimo. The duties of your office are sacred and important, and will require your attendance at every Conclave. And may He who is able, abundantly furnish you for every good work, preserve you from falling into error, improve, strengthen, establish and perfect you; and finally greet you with, "Well done, *thou* good and faithful servant: enter thou into the joy of thy Lord."

CHARGE TO THE GRAND SENIOR WARDEN.

Eminent Sir, you have been elected Grand Senior Warden in this Grand Commandery, and I now invest you with the Jewel of your office. Your station is at the Southwest angle of the Triangle. Let it be your constant care that the Warrior be not deterred from duty, nor the Penitent molested on his journey.

CHARGE TO THE GRAND JUNIOR WARDEN.

Eminent Sir, having been elected Grand Junior Warden, I now invest you with the Jewel of your office. Your station is at the Northwest angle of the Triangle. Your duty will be to attend on all visiting Knights, and, if found worthy, to introduce them, on the order of the Grand Commander, into the Asylum. Be ye therefore perfect, always abounding in the work of the Lord.

CHARGE TO THE GRAND TREASURER.

Eminent Sir, you have been elected Treasurer of the Grand Commandery, and I now invest you with the Jewel of your office.

Your station is on the right, in front of the Grand Generalissimo. The qualities that should especially distinguish the incumbent of your station are accuracy and fidelity—accuracy, in keeping a fair and minute account of all receipts and disbursements; fidelity, in carefully preserving all the property and funds of the Grand Commandery that may lawfully come into your hands, and rendering a just account of the same whenever called upon. Your respect for and attachment to this Grand Commandery and the great Order of the Temple, will stimulate you to a zealous, faithful, and prompt discharge of the trust confided to you.

CHARGE TO THE GRAND RECORDER.

Eminent Sir, by the suffrages of the Grand Commandery you have been chosen Grand Recorder, and I now invest you with the Jewel of your office. In selecting you to discharge the duties of this most important trust, the Sir Knights have been guided by a belief that you possess in a large degree the qualities that should distinguish a Grand Recorder. I can not doubt your resolve to discharge these important duties with benefit to this Grand Commandery, and with honor to yourself. Your station, to which you will now repair, is on the left, and in front, of the Grand Captain General.

CHARGE TO THE GRAND STANDARD BEARER.

Eminent Sir, to you has been awarded the distinction of Grand Standard Bearer, and I now invest you with the Jewel appropriate to that office. Your station is in the West. Your duty is to display, support, and protect the Banner of our Order, which I now place in your official custody. Let your conduct be such that the virtuous will delight to imitate it.

CHARGE TO THE GRAND SWORD BEARER.

Eminent Sir, having been elected Grand Sword Bearer, I now invest you with the Jewel of your office. Your station is on the right of the Grand Standard Bearer. You are to assist in the protection of the Banner of our Order with that mystic Sword which is endowed with justice and tempered by mercy.

CHARGE TO THE GRAND WARDER.

Eminent Sir, the Grand Commandery has selected you to fill the office of Grand Warder, and I now invest you with the Jewel of your office. Your station is on the left of the Grand Standard Bearer. Your duty is to announce the approach of the Grand Commander, and to announce all visiting Sir Knights who may be admitted to the privileges of our Conclaves. You will therefore be punctual, and by a strict performance of duty merit not only the honor now conferred upon you, but the commendation of all Sir Knights who may experience your official courtesy.

CHARGE TO THE GRAND CAPTAIN OF THE GUARD.

Eminent Sir, you have been elected to the responsible station of Grand Captain of the Guard, and I now invest you with the Jewel appropriate to your office. Holding the post of danger and of honor, your vigilance should be sleepless, your courage undaunted, and your courtesy beyond question. See to it that the avenues of approach are strictly guarded. Your courage should keep the unworthy at bay, but the valiant and the true should receive from you the knightly welcome due to a Soldier of the Cross.

GC.–Sir Knight Grand Marshal, make Proclamation in the East.

G. MAR.–Sir Knights, ATTENTION! In the name and by authority of the Grand Commandery of Knights Templar of the State of –, I proclaim the Officers thereof duly elected and installed.

GC.–Grand Commandery, BE SEATED!

INSTALLATION OF GRAND ENCAMPMENT.

The Grand Encampment has adopted only the Vow to be taken by its Officers, but certain ceremonies are usually observed in administering that Vow, and in installing each into his office. The following is offered to the consideration of the Grand Encampment at its Conclave of 1895:

GM.–Sir Knights, your Grand Master, and the other Grand Officers whom you have chosen, are in readiness for installation. The Grand Marshal will announce to them our readiness to install the Grand Master, and he will escort the Grand Master and the Officers elect to the East.

The Grand Marshal repairs to the room in which the Officers elect are assembled, and will escort them, in single file, to the Asylum. When they reach the door of the Asylum—

GW.–The Grand Master elect, and his associate Officers, approach.

The Grand Master calls up the Grand Encampment; a March is played as they pass down the Asylum, and halt in the East, in front of chairs prepared as seats for them.

G. MAR.—Most Eminent Grand Master, the Grand Officers elect are before you, and await your pleasure.

GM.—Excellent Grand Prelate, lead us in a solemn Invocation to the Throne of Grace. Sir Knights, UNCOVER!

The Grand Prelate will offer the following, or some other appropriate:

PRAYER.

OUR FATHER, who art in Heaven, bow down Thine ear, we beseech Thee, and hearken unto the voice of our supplication. Pardon our sins, and blot our transgressions, and give unto each of us a broken and a contrite spirit.

Give unto these, Thy servants, whom we have chosen to rule over us, wisdom from on high. Give unto each the spirit of the Master, and may the words of their mouths and the meditations of their hearts be acceptable in Thy sight, through Jesus Christ, our Lord, and our Redeemer. AMEN!

GM.—Sir Knights, RE-COVER! Officers elect, before I can install you into your respective stations, I must receive from you a solemn Vow to be faithful to the trust about to be reposed in you. Most Eminent Grand Master elect, are you ready to take such a Vow?

He answers in the affirmative.

GM.—Very Eminent Deputy Grand Master, are you so ready?

He answers in the affirmative.

GM.–Are you all so ready?

They all say, each for himself, "I am".

GM.–Let the Grand Master elect approach the East.

Grand Marshal escorts him to the East.

GM.–Most Eminent Sir, you will now uncover, place your right hand upon your heart, and repeat after me:

The Grand Master uncovers.

I, –, do promise and vow that I will support and maintain the Constitution and Statutes of the Grand Encampment of Knights Templar of the United States of America, and will use my best endeavors to cause a proper observance of the same, according to the authority which is in me vested; and that I will, to the best of my ability, faithfully discharge the duties pertaining to the office to which I have been elected.

GM.–Most Eminent Sir, I now with pleasure invest you with the Jewel of your high office, the highest in the gift of the great Order of the Temple.

The GM. takes the Jewel from his own breast, goes down and places it on the breast of the new Grand Master.

GM.–One so distinguished in the Order needs no admonition from me as to how this Jewel should be worn. The interests of the Order are placed in your hands, whether for weal or woe depends upon the fulfillment of the promises you have made to yourself, and to us. This body, whose chief you now are, feels confident that you will not abuse or pervert the powers conferred upon you as Grand Master.

It is known to you that to rule *well* has not been the lot of all called to such duty. And it is further known to you that it is not by a strong arm, or by an iron will, that order and obedience are secured, but by holding the *key* to the hearts of men. We hope and believe that you now and ever will hold such a key.

You will ascend to your station in the Grand East, and receive the salutations of your Companions-in- arms.

The Grand Master is escorted to his chair by the Grand Marshal. He stands in his station.

GM.—Most Eminent Sir, I now salute you, and proclaim you Grand Master of the Grand Encampment of Knights Templar of the United States of America!

GM.—Sir Knights, Behold your Grand Master!

The Grand Encampment will salute with the sign of the Order. The new Grand Master will make such remarks as he desires.

IN. OF.—Most Eminent Grand Master, the remaining Officers elect await your pleasure.

The Grand Master will install the remainder of the Officers, or he may ask the Installing Officer to continue.

GM.—Sir Knights, BE SEATED!

IN. OF.—Officers elect, ATTENTION! Place your right hands upon your hearts, uncover, and repeat after me:

Same Vow as that taken by the Grand Master.

IN. OF.—Present the Deputy Grand Master, and the remaining Officers elect will be seated.

G. MAR.—Most Eminent Sir, I present Very Eminent Sir —, who has been chosen Deputy Grand Master, and is now ready for installation.

IN. OF.—Very Eminent Sir, you are aware that in case of incapacity of the Grand Master to act, you are to succeed to his duties. Remember that you are placed in most intimate relations with him, as head of the Order.

I now invest you with the Jewel of your office, and the Grand Marshal will conduct you to your station, on the right of the Most Eminent Grand Master.

The Grand Marshal will present the remaining Grand Officers as the Installing Officer may direct.

GRAND GENERALISSIMO AND GRAND CAPTAIN GENERAL.

IN. OF.—Invest the Eminent Fratres with the Jewels of their offices. (*Done by Grand Marshal.*) Sir Knights, repair to your stations, and be not weary in well doing, for in due season you shall reap if you faint not!

THE GRAND WARDENS.

IN. OF.—Invest the Eminent Fratres with the Jewels of their offices. (*Done.*) Sir Knights, repair to your stations, and see that the courtesies of the Grand Encampment are extended to all worthy visiting Knights of the Order of the Temple.

THE GRAND TREASURER AND GRAND RECORDER.

IN. OF.—Sir Knights, you have been chosen to responsible stations, because the Grand Encampment believed you worthy and competent. See to it that their confidence has been well reposed. Repair to your stations.

STANDARD BEARER, SWORD BEARER, AND WARDER.

IN. OF.—Place the Grand Standard in possession of its new Bearer. (*Done.*) Sir Knight, bear it worthily, and so display its precious emblem—in which Sign we shall all conquer—that each valiant Knight may be prompted to exclaim in the words of its gracious inscription, "Not unto us, O Lord; not unto us, but unto thy Name be the glory."

And you, Sir Knight Sword Bearer, protect that Banner at peril of your life. And if, in the vicissitudes of the next three years, it should fall from the hands of its Bearer, raise it aloft, for unto that honor you temporarily succeed.

Sir Knight Warder, be vigilant in the discharge of your responsible duties. Look well to the avenues of the Asylum, and see that all are duly guarded.

Sir Knights, repair to your stations, and remember that zeal and vigilance are necessary prerequisites to your offices.

IN. OF.—The Grand Marshal will make Proclamation. Grand Encampment, ATTENTION!

G. MAR.—In the name and by the authority of the Grand Encampment of Knights Templar of the United States of America, I now proclaim the Officers thereof duly elected and installed. GM.—Grand Encampment, BE SEATED!

TEMPLAR UNIFORM.

EDICT OF 1886.

1. The Uniform of Knights Templar, Knights of Malta, and Knights of the Red Cross, under the immediate jurisdiction of the Grand Encampment, is that prescribed by the Grand Encampment. No other Uniform is allowed, except in case of Washington Commandery, No. 1, of District of Columbia, whose members are permitted to wear the Uniform prescribed and worn in that Commandery before the adoption of the regulation of 1882.

2. Each Grand Commandery shall have full power and authority to prescribe the Uniform to be worn by those belonging to its own jurisdiction, except that the Insignia of Rank shall always be under the exclusive control and regulation of the Grand Encampment, and no other authority shall alter, modify, or in any way interfere therewith.

INSIGNIA OF OFFICE.

TO BE FOREVER UNDER THE EXCLUSIVE CONTROL OF THE GRAND ENCAMPMENT.

SHOULDER STRAPS.

EDICT OF 1892.

For the Grand Master, and Past Grand Masters of Grand Encampment:

Royal purple silk velvet, two inches wide by four inches long (outside measurement), bordered with two rows of embroidery, of gold, three-eighths of an inch wide; the Cross of Salem embroidered, of gold, in the center, lengthwise.

For all other Grand Officers of the Grand Encampment:

The same as the Grand Master, except for the Cross of Salem the Patriarchal Cross, of gold, with the initials of the office, respectively, embroidered, of silver (Old English characters), at the foot of the Cross, narrowwise of the Strap.

For Officers and Past Grand Officers of Grand Commanderies, except Past Grand Commanders:

Bright red silk velvet, two inches wide by four inches long, bordered with one row of embroidery, of gold, a quarter of an inch wide; the Templar's Cross, of gold, with the initials of the office, respectively, to be embroidered (Old English characters) in silver on the lower end of the Strap.

For Past Grand Commanders:

The same as above, except that the color of the Shoulder Strap shall be royal purple, and the lettering omitted.

For the Commander of a Subordinate Commandery:

Emerald green silk velvet, one and a half inches wide by four inches long, bordered with one row of embroidery, of gold, one-quarter of an inch wide; the Passion Cross, with a halo, embroidered, of silver, in the center.

For Past Commanders of Subordinate Commanderies:

The same as for Commanders, except that the color of the Strap shall be bright red.

For the Generalissimo of a Subordinate Commandery:

Same as the Commander, except for the Passion Cross the Square, surmounted with the Paschal Lamb.

For the Captain General of a Subordinate Commandery:

Same as the Commander, except for the Passion Cross the Level, surmounted with the Cock.

CROSSES.

Commanders and Past Commanders will wear the Passion Cross.

Grand and Past Grand Officers of Grand Commanderies will wear the Templar Cross.

BURIAL SERVICE.

GENERAL REGULATIONS.

1. No Knight Templar can be buried with the funeral honors of Knighthood, unless he be in regular standing.

2. It is the duty of the Eminent Commander to convene the Commandery, upon notice of the death of a Sir Knight who may be entitled to receive funeral honors, upon request, made when living or by his family after his decease, for the purpose of attending the funeral ceremonies.

3. The Knights, on such occasions, will attend in full uniform, pursuant to the regulations; their sword hilts and the Banner of the Commandery suitably dressed in mourning.

4. On the coffin of the deceased will be placed his hat and sword; and if an Officer, his jewel, trimmed with crape.

5. The Eminent Commander will preside during the services, and, assisted by the Prelate, lead in the ceremonies, pursuant to the Ritual. If Grand Officers or Past Grand Officers be present, they will be allotted a place in the procession according to their rank.

6. The Knights will assemble at their Asylum, and march to the residence of the deceased, in the usual order of processions, swords at Carry; the line being headed by the Warder, and the Officers being in the rear, according to rank; that is, the Eminent Commander last.

The military movements necessary to the Burial Service will be conducted according to the Tactics of the Jurisdiction.

When desirable, the part of the service set down for the "Residence or the Church" may be deferred until the procession reaches the grave.

During the reading of the Scriptures, and during Prayer, all will Uncover without commands or signals, and Re-cover at conclusions.

If it is inconvenient to form the Triangle at the grave, the Commandery can be formed in two lines, one on each side of the grave, the Commander and Prelate at the head, pall-bearers beside the coffin, and mourners and friends at the foot.

The Ritual directs that the body be lowered into the grave immediately after the address by the Prelate, and when the Junior Warden removes the sword from the coffin. It has been the practice of the author of this MONITOR to not lower the coffin until the service was concluded, and the Lord's Prayer repeated. Then, while being lowered, to sing a hymn, which always proved a great relief to the mourners, as well as adding to the solemnities of the entire service.

It is effective to have the "Responses" made, in unison, by the Generalissimo and Captain General, only.

THE RITUAL.

AT THE RESIDENCE, OR IN THE CHURCH.

EC.—Sir Knights, in the solemn rites of our Order, we have often been reminded of the fact that we were born to die. Mortality has been brought to view, that we might more earnestly seek an immortality beyond this fleeting life, where death comes no more forever. The sad and mournful knell has betokened that another spirit has winged its flight to a new existence. An alarm has come to the door of our Asylum, and the messenger was Death. None presumed to say to the awful presence: "Who dares approach?" A pilgrim warrior has been summoned, "and there is no discharge in that war." A burning taper of life in our Commandery has been extinguished, and none save the High and Holy One can re- light it. All that remains of our beloved companion lies mute before us, and the light of the eye, and the breathing of the lips, in fraternal greeting, has ceased to us forever on this side of the grave. His Sword, vowed to be drawn in the cause of truth, justice, and liberty, only, reposes in its scabbard, and we can no longer shield him from wrong and oppression.

The Knights here return Swords without command, on the signal of the Eminent Commander.

It is meet, at such a time, that we should be silent, and allow the words of the Infinite and Undying to speak, that we may gather consolation from His revelations, and have impressed upon our minds lessons of wisdom, instruction, and the meetness of preparation for the last great change which must pass upon us all.

Let us be reverently attentive while our Prelate reads unto us a lesson from the Holy Scriptures. P.—Help, Lord: for the faithful fail from among the children of men.

RES.—Help us, O Lord.

P.—*The righteous* cry, and the Lord heareth, and delivereth them out of all their troubles. RES.—Hear us, O Lord.

P.—The Lord *is* nigh unto them that are of a broken heart: and saveth such as be of a contrite spirit. RES.—Be nigh unto us, O Lord.

P.—The Lord redeemeth the soul of his servants: and none of them that trust in Him shall be desolate. RES.—Redeem us, O Lord.

P.—For I will not trust in my bow, neither shall my sword save me. RES.—Redeem us, O Lord.

P.—But God will redeem my soul from the power of the grave: for he shall receive me. RES.—Redeem us, O Lord.

P.—Wilt thou shew wonders to the dead? Shall the dead arise *and* praise thee? Shall thy lovingkindness be declared in the grave? *or* thy faithfulness in destruction?

RES.—Save us, O Lord.

P.—We spend our years as a tale *that is told.* The days of our years *are* threescore years and ten; and if by reason of strength *they be* fourscore years, yet *is* their strength labor and sorrow; for it is soon cut off, and we fly away. So teach *us* to number our days, that we may apply *our* hearts unto wisdom.

RES.—Teach us, O Lord.

P.—For he knoweth our frame; he remembereth that we *are* dust. As *for* man, his days *are* as grass: as a flower of the field, so he flourisheth. For the wind passeth over it, and it is gone; and the place thereof shall know it no more. But the mercy of the Lord *is* from everlasting to everlasting upon them that fear him.

RES.—Show mercy, O Lord.

P.—We shall not all sleep, but we shall all be changed, In a moment, in the twinkling of an eye, at the last trump: for the trumpet shall sound, and the dead shall be raised incorruptible, and we shall be changed. For this corruptible must put on incorruption, and this mortal *must* put on immortality. So when this corruptible shall have put on in-

corruption, and this mortal shall have put on immortality, then shall be brought to pass the saying that is written, Death is swallowed up in victory. O death, where is thy sting? O grave, where *is* thy victory?

RES.—O death, where is thy sting? O grave, where is thy victory?

P.—The sting of death *is* sin; and the strength of sin *is* the law. But thanks *be* to God, which giveth us the victory through our Lord Jesus Christ..

RES.—Thanks be unto God.

EC.—Shall the memory of our departed brother fade from among men? RES.—It is cherished in our souls forever.

EC.—Shall no record be left of his virtues and worth?

RES.—It is inscribed upon our hearts; it is written in our archives; the heart may cease to throb, and the archives may moulder and decay, but the tablets of the Recording Angel on high can never perish.

The Recorder here opens the Book of Records of the Commandery, on which a page is set apart, suitably inscribed, and says:

RECORDER.—Thus it is written.

The Knights bow their heads.

EC.—He was a true and courteous Knight, and has fallen in life's struggle full knightly, with his armor on.

P.—Rest to his ashes and peace to his soul.

RES.—Rest to his ashes and peace to his soul.

P.—Sovereign Ruler of the Universe! into thy hands we devoutly and submissively commit the departed spirit.

RES.—Thy will be done, O God.

A Hymn will then be sung.
The following, or an extemporaneous, Prayer will then be
made by the Prelate, or by any clergyman present:

FATHER OF LIGHT, in this dark and trying hour of calamity and sorrow, we humbly lift our hearts to Thee. Give us, we pray, that light which cometh down from above. Thou hast mercifully said in Thy holy word, that the bruised reed Thou wouldst not break; remember in mercy, O Lord, these bereaved ones now before Thee. [Be Thou, at this hour, the Father of the fatherless, and the widow's God.

Administer to them the consolations which they so sorely need.] Cause us to look away from these sad scenes of frail mortality to the hopes which lie beyond the grave, and bind us yet closer together in the ties of brotherly love and affection. While we see how frail is man, and how uncertain the continuance of our lives upon the earth, and are reminded of our own mortality, lead us, by Thy grace and spirit, to turn our thoughts to those things which make for our everlasting peace; and give us a frame of mind to make a proper improvement of all the admonitions of thy providence, and fix our thoughts more devotedly on Thee,

the only sure refuge in time of need. And at last, when our earthly pilgrimage shall be ended, or ever the silver cord be loosed, or the golden bowl be broken, wilt Thou, in that moment of mortal extremity be indeed *Emmanuel*—God with us! May the lamp of Thy love dispel the gloom of the dark valley, and may we be enabled by the intercession of Thy Son, to gain admission into the blessed Asylum above; and in Thy glorious presence, enjoy a union with the spirits of the departed, perfect as is the happiness of heaven, and durable as the eternity of God. AMEN!
RES.—AMEN AND AMEN!

All Re-cover.
The procession will then form and march to the place of interment, in the same order as before.

AT THE GRAVE.

On arriving at the place, while forming in order, a suitable Dirge may be played by the band.
The Knights will form, if convenient, a Triangle around the grave, the base being at the foot, the Eminent Commander and Prelate being at the head, and the friends and relatives at the foot. If a Triangle is inconvenient, form in two lines on the sides of the grave.

P.—Sir Knights, there is one sacred spot upon the earth where the footfalls of our march are unheeded; our trumpets quicken no pulse and incite no fear; the rustling of our banners and the gleam of our swords awaken no emotion. It is the silent city of the dead where we now stand. Awe rests upon every heart, and the stern warrior's eyes are bedewed with feelings which never shame his manhood. It needs no siege, nor assault, nor beleaguering host to enter its walls; we fear no sortie, and listen for no battle shout. No Warder's challenge greets the ear, nor do we wait awhile with patience for permission to enter.

Hither must we all come at last; and the stoutest heart and the manliest form that surrounds me will then be led a captive, without title or rank, in the chains of mortality and the habiliments of slavery to the King of Terrors.

But if he has been faithful to the Captain of his Salvation, a true Soldier of the Cross; if he has offered suitable gifts at the shrine of his departed Lord, and bears the signet of the Lion of the Tribe of Judah, then play he claim to be of that princely house and to be admitted to audience with the Sovereign Master of Heaven and Earth. Then will he be stripped of the chains of earthly captivity and clothed in a white garment, glistening as the sun, and be seated with princes and rulers, and partake of a libation, not of death and sorrow, but of that wine which is drunk forever new in the Father's kingdom above.

We can not come here without subdued hearts and softened affections. Often as the challenge conies which takes from our side some loved associate, some cherished companion-in-arms, and often as the trumpet sounds its wailing notes to summon us to the death-bed and the brink of the sepulchre, we can not contemplate "the last of earth" unmoved. Each successive death-note snaps some fiber which binds us to this lower existence and makes us pause and reflect upon that dark and gloomy chamber where we must all terminate our pilgrimage. Well will it be for our peace then, if we can wash our hands, not only in token of sincerity, but of every guilty stain, and give honest and satisfactory answers to the questions required.

The sad and solemn scene now before us stirs up these recollections with a force and vivid power which we have hitherto unfelt. He who now slumbers in that last, long, unbroken sleep of death was our brother. With him have we walked the pilgrimage of life and kept ward and watch together in its vicissitudes and trials. He is now removed beyond the effect of our praise or censure. That we loved him our presence here evinces; and we remember him in scenes to which the world was not witness, and where the better feelings of humanity were exhibited without disguise. That he had faults and foibles is but to repeat what his mortality demonstrates—that he had a human nature, not divine. Over these errors, whatever they may have been, we cast, while living, the mantle of charity; it should, with much more reason, enshroud him in death. We who have been taught to extend the point of charity even to a foe when fallen, can not be severe or merciless toward a loved brother.

The memory of his virtues lingers in our remembrance and reflects its shining lustre beyond the portals of the tomb. The earthen vase which has contained precious odors will lose none of its fragrance, though the clay be broken and shattered. So be it with our brother's memory.

The Junior Warden removes the Sword from the coffin, which will then be lowered into the grave, while the Prelate repeats as follows: (See General Regulations for a different ceremony.)

P.—I am the resurrection, and the life: he that believeth in me, though he were dead, yet shall he live: and whosoever liveth and believeth in me shall never die. To the earth we commit the mortal remains of our deceased brother,—we have already commended his soul to his Creator,—with humble submission to Divine Providence. (*Here cast some earth on the coffin.*) Earth to earth (*cast earth again*); ashes to ashes (*cast more earth*); dust to dust— till the morn of the resurrection, when, like our risen and ascended Redeemer, he shall break the bonds of death, and abide the judgment of the great day. Till then, Friend, Brother, Sir Knight, farewell! Light lie the ashes upon thee, and may the sunshine of heaven beam bright on thy waking!

RES.—AMEN AND AMEN!

The Junior Warden presents the Sword to the Eminent Commander, who says:

EC.—Our departed brother was taught, while living, that this Sword, in his hands, as a true and courteous Knight, was endowed with three most estimable qualities: Its hilt with *justice* impartial; its blade with *fortitude* undaunted; and its point with *mercy* unrestrained. To these lessons, with their deep emblematical significance, we trust he gave diligent heed. He could never grasp its hilt without being reminded of the lively significance of the attributes it inculcated. He has borne the pangs of dissolving nature,—may we trust that with the same *fortitude* he sustained the trials of this passing existence. To his name and memory be *justice* done, as we hope to receive the like justice ourselves. And may that *mercy* unrestrained, which is the glorious attribute of the Son of God, interpose in his behalf to parry the sword of Divine Justice, and to admit him to the blessed companionship of saints and angels in the realms of light and life eternal.

RES.—AMEN AND AMEN!

The Senior Warden presents a Cross to the Prelate, who says:

P.—This symbol of faith—the Christian's hope and the Christian's trust—we again place upon the breast of our brother, there to remain till the last trumpet shall sound and earth and sea yield up their dead. Though it may, in the past history of our race, have been perverted into an ensign of oppression and wrong; though it may have been made the emblem of fraud and superstition and moral darkness, its true significance remained,— the badge of the Christian warrior. To-day it calls to mind Gethsemane and its sorrowful garden; the judgment hall of Pilate and the pitiless crown of thorns; Golgotha and Calvary, and their untold agonies, that fallen man might live and inherit everlasting life. If an inspired apostle was not ashamed of the Cross, neither should we be; if he gloried in the significance of the truths it shadowed forth, so ought we to rejoice in it as the speaking witness of our reliance beyond the grave. May this hope of the living have been the anchor to the soul of our departed brother—the token to admit him to that peaceful haven where the wicked cease from troubling and the weary are at rest.

Res.—Amen and Amen!

The Prelate drops the Cross into the grave, or lays it on the coffin, and continues:

P.—The Orders of Christian Knighthood were instituted in a dark period of the world's history, but their mission was high and holy. To succor and protect the sorrowing and destitute, the innocent and oppressed, was their vow and their life-long labor and duty. For long, long years they well and nobly performed their vows and did their devoirs. In those rude ages the steel blade was oftener the arbiter of justice than the judgments of judicial tribunals or the decrees of magistrates. So long as the

Templars adhered to their vows of poverty they were virtuous and innocent, and their language was in truth, "Silver and gold have I none; but such as I have give I thee." But, with the accession of wealth and civil power, they were tempted, and fell from their high estate, and their possessions attracted the cupidity and their prowess incurred the hatred of the despots of those times. When the martyred De Molai had perished and the Order was proscribed, they united with the fraternity of Free and Accepted Masons, and returned to their primitive simplicity of manners; and a rough habit, coarse diet and severe duty was all that was offered to their votaries.

In our land we have perpetuated only the distinctive rites, with the appellations and regulations of the defenders of the Holy Sepulchre—the early champions and soldiers of the Cross—and this as a guerdon of merit, not a badge of rank. The Sword in our hands is more as a symbol of the duties we have vowed to fulfill than an instrument of assault or defense. We claim to exercise practical virtues in the holy bonds of our confraternity, in humble imitation of those renowned Knights of the olden time; for there is still in this refined age innocence to be guarded, widowed hearts to be relieved of their burdens, and orphanage to be protected from the chill blasts of a wintry world; and to be true and courteous is not limited to any age or clime.

Our brother, whose cold and lifeless remains have just been committed to the earth, was one of our fraternal band, bound by the same ties and pledged to the same duties. To his bereaved and mourning friends and relatives we have but little worldly consolation to offer, but we do tender them our heartfelt sympathies. And if the solemn and interesting ceremonies in which we

have been engaged have not pointed them to a higher hope and
a better consolation, then all our condolence would be in vain.

Sir Knight Companions, let us pray.

Here all repeat the LORD'S PRAYER.
The Prelate will then pronounce the following:

BENEDICTION.

The grace of the Lord Jesus Christ, and the love of God, and
the communion of the Holy Ghost, be with you all. AMEN!

*Lines are reformed, and the Commandery returns to the
Asylum.*

THE ORDER OF MALTA,

OR

KNIGHT HOSPITALER,
OF THE ORDER OF
SAINT JOHN OF JERUSALEM, PALESTINE, RHODES AND MALTA.

*According to the Ritual Adopted
by Grand Encampment in 1883.*

TO OPEN A PRIORY.

ALL being suitably equipped, and the Priory suitably arrayed, the necessary precautionary steps will be taken. This is the array:

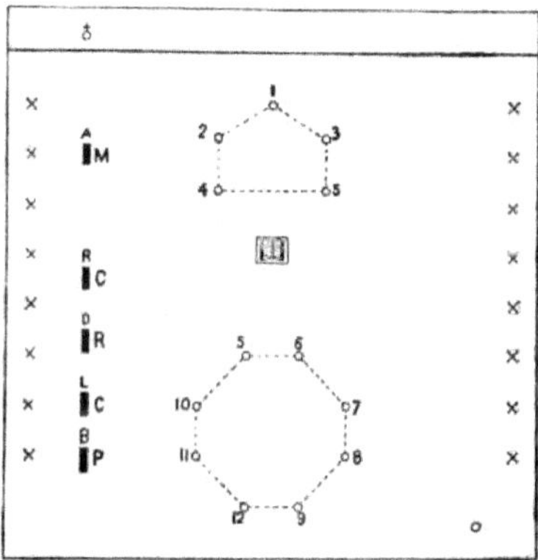

KNIGHT OF SAINT PAUL.

* * * *
* *

PAUL AT MELITA (MALTA).

And when they were escaped, then they knew that the island was called Melita. And the barbarous people shewed us no little kindness: for they kindled a fire, and received us every one, because of the present rain, and because of the cold. And when Paul had gathered a bundle of sticks, and laid *them* on the fire, there came a viper out of the heat, and fastened on his hand. And when the barbarians saw the *venomous* beast hang on his hand, they said among themselves, No doubt this man is a murderer, whom, though he hath escaped the sea, yet vengeance suffereth not to live. And he shook off the beast into the fire, and felt no harm. Howbeit they looked when he should have swollen, or fallen down dead suddenly: but after they had looked a great while, and saw no harm come to him, they changed their minds, and said that he was a god. Acts xxviii: 1-6.

* * * *
* *

PAUL'S EXHORTATION.

And now I exhort you to be of good cheer: for there shall be no loss of *any man's* life among you, but of the ship. For there stood by me this night the angel of God, whose I am, and whom I serve, saying, Fear not, Paul; thou must be brought before Cæsar: and, lo, God hath given thee all them that sail with thee. Wherefore, sirs, be of good cheer: for I believe God, that it shall be even as it was told me. Acts xxvii: 22-25.

```
*    *      *    *
   *          *
```

F N. P.

```
*    *      *    *
   *          *
```

KNIGHT HOSPITALER.

```
*    *      *    *
   *          *
```

B. L. D. R. A.

```
*    *      *    *
   *          *
```

VOW.

```
*    *      *    *
   *          *
```

Admitted.   Raised.

```
*    *      *    *
   *          *
```

THE BEATITUDES.

Blessed *are* the poor in spirit: for their's is the kingdom of heaven. Blessed *are* they that mourn: for they shall be comforted. Blessed *are* the meek: for they shall inherit the earth. Blessed *are* they which do hunger and thirst after righteousness: for they shall be filled. Blessed *are* the merciful: for they shall obtain mercy. Blessed *are* the pure in heart: for they shall see God. Blessed *are* the peacemakers: for they shall be called the children of God. Blessed *are* they which *are* persecuted for righteousness' sake: for their's is the kingdom of heaven. Blessed are ye, when *men* shall revile you, and persecute *you*, and shall say all manner of evil against you falsely, for my sake. Matt. v: 3-11.

*　　*　　　*　　*
*　　　　*

DOUBTING THOMAS.

But Thomas, one of the twelve, called Didymus, was not with them when Jesus came. The other disciples therefore said unto him, We have seen the Lord. But he said unto them, Except I shall see in his hands the print of the nails, and put my finger into the print of the nails, and thrust my hand into his side, I will not believe. And after eight days again his disciples were within, and Thomas with them: then came Jesus, the doors being shut, and stood in the midst, and said, Peace *be* unto you. Then saith he to Thomas, Reach hither thy finger, and behold my hands; and reach hither thy hand, and thrust *it* into my side; and be not faithless, but believing. And Thomas answered and said unto him, My Lord and my God. John xx: 24-28.+

* * * *
* *

THE INSCRIPTION.

And Pilate wrote a title, and put *it* on the cross. And the writing was, JESUS OF NAZARETH THE KING OF THE JEWS. John xix: 19. Here endeth the third lesson.

* * * *
* *

RECOGNITION.

* * * *
* *

NOTE.—As a new ORDER OF MALTA will (D. V.) be submitted to the Grand Encampment, at its Triennial, Boston, 1893, the above will be sufficient for the Commanderies at present.

FLOOR PLAN
OF THE PROPOSED REVISED RITUAL OF THE ORDER OF MALTA.

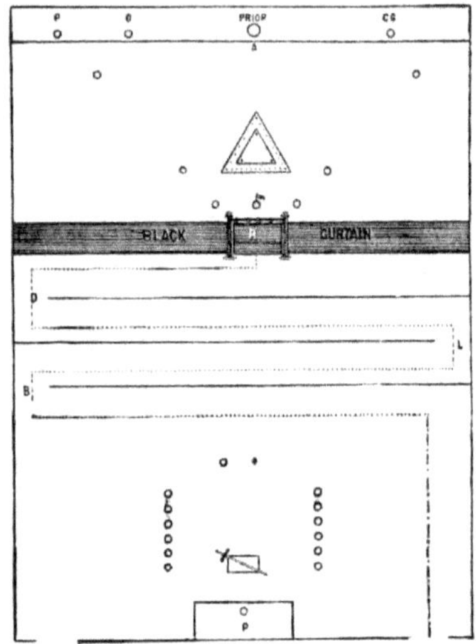

Stations same as in K. T. at Opening. The dotted lines show course of second entrance.

This plan contemplates the use of a single Hall, which is most desirable. The Bulwarks are Cyprus, Rhodes, and Malta. Meditations at these are on the Birth, Life, Death, Resurrection and Ascension of our Saviour.

SECOND APPENDIX

ANNO DOMINI.

The Christian Era was first used by a Roman abbot, Denys le Petit, or Dionisius Exigus, about the year 527. It was generally adopted in England in the eighth century. The Council of Chelsea, July, 816, ordained that all bishops should date their acts from the year of the incarnation of our Saviour. In the Eastern Empire it was not in general use until after the capture of Constantinople by Mahomet II, in 1453.

Down to 1752 the Historical year in England commenced on January 1st, and the Ecclesiastical, Civil (Legal) year commenced on March 25th. This led to great confusion, to avoid which it was long the custom to add the date of the *Historical* to that of the *Legal* year, when speaking of any day between January 1st and March 25th, thus:

$$\text{January 30, 164}\begin{cases}8 & \textit{i. e.,}\ 1648,\ \text{the Civil (Legal) year.}\\ 9 & \textit{i. e.,}\ 1649,\ \text{the Historical year.}\end{cases}$$

Others wrote it thus: January. 30, 1645-9. The lower, or last, figure always indicated the year according to the present calculation.

MASONIC CALENDARS.

The various bodies of Freemasonry have adopted Calendars for their special use. In the following table the figures are carried out for the year 1893.

KNIGHTS TEMPLAR founded 1118. Hence *Anno Ordinis* 775. SECOND TEMPLE began to be built by Zerubbabel, B. C. 330.

Hence the ROYAL ARCH, *Anno Inventionis* (Year of Discovery) 2423. ROYAL AND SELECT MASTERS refer to completion of the Temple, 1000 B. C. Hence R. AND A. MASTERS, *Anno Depositionis* (Year of Deposit) 2893.

ANCIENT CRAFT MASONS use *Anno Lucis* (Year of Light)–Creation 5893. SCOTTISH RITE uses *Anno Mundi* (Year of World)–Creation 5653.

THE MOON'S RISING AND SETTING.

At 4 days old the moon sets at about 10 at night.

At 5 days old at about 11 at night. At 6 days old at about 12 at night.

At 7 days old at or near I in morning.

At 15 days old at full it rises about 6 in evening. At 16 days old at a quarter past 7 in evening.

At 17 days old at half past 8 in evening. At IS days old about Lo at night.

At 19 clays old about 11 at night. At 20 days old about 12 at night.

THE DIVISION OF TIME.

DAYS OF THE WEEK.

SUNDAY (Anglo-Saxon, *Sunnandæg*), day of the sun. MONDAY (Anglo-Saxon, *Monandæg*), day of the moon.

TUESDAY (Anglo-Saxon, *Tiwesdæg*), from Tiw, the god of war. WEDNESDAY (Anglo-Saxon, *Wodnesdæg*), from Odin, the god of storms. THURSDAY (Anglo-Saxon, *Thunresdæg*), day of Thor, the god of thunder. FRIDAY (Anglo-Saxon, *Frigedæg*), day of Freya, goddess of marriage.

SATURDAY (Anglo-Saxon, *Saterdæg;* Latin, *Dies Saturnus*), day of Saturn, the god of time.

The Chinese and Thibetans have a week of five days, named after iron, wood, water, feathers and earth.

NAMES OF THE MONTHS.

JANUARY.—The Roman Janus presided over the beginning of everything; hence the first month of the year was called after him.

FEBRUARY (Latin, *Februarius*).—The month of purification; on the 15th day of this month the Feast of Expiation was held.

MARCH.—Named from the Roman god of war, Mars.

APRIL, (Latin, *Aprilis*).—Probably derived from *aperire*, to open; because spring generally begins and the buds open in this month.

MAY (Latin, *Maius*).—From Maia, a feminine divinity worshiped at Rome on the Ist day of this month. JUNE.—From Juno, a Roman divinity worshiped as the queen of heaven.

JULY (*Julius*). Julius Cæsar was born in this month.

AUGUST.—Named by the Emperor Augustus Cæsar, B. C. 30, after himself. He regarded it as a fortunate month, being that in which he had gained several victories.

SEPTEMBER (*Septem,* or seven).—September was the seventh month in the old Roman calendar. OCTOBER (*Octo,* or eight).—Eighth month of the old Roman year.

NOVEMBER (*Novem,* or nine).—November was the ninth month in the old Roman year.

DECEMBER (*Decem,* or ten).—December was the tenth month of the early Roman year. About the twenty-first of this month the sun enters the Tropic of Capricorn, and forms the winter solstice.

THE YEAR.

The Solar or astronomical year was, 265 years B. C., determined to comprise 365 days, 5 hours, 48 minutes, 51 seconds. The *Lunar* year, comprehending 12 moons, or 354 days, 8 hours, 48 minutes, was the regulator of time among the Chaldeans, Persians and Jews. Till the time of William the Conqueror the English began their year on the 25th of December. Down to 1732 the year did not legally commence till the 25th of March. In Scotland, at that date, the year began on the 1st of January.

To adjust the Calendar, a new one was published by Pope Gregory XIII in 1582, omitting ten days, the 5th of October becoming the 15th. The New Style was not adopted in Great Britain till 1752, when eleven days were jumped, the 3d of September being reckoned the 14th. In Russia and the East the Old Style is still in force, and all Russian dates are twelve days earlier than English.

THE NAME OF GOD IN TWENTY-TWO LANGUAGES.

Assyrian, *Eleah;* Celtic, *Diu;* Chinese, *Prussa;* Arabic, *Allah;* Dutch, *Godt;* Danish, *Gut;* English, *God;* French, *Dieu;* Greek, *Theos;* Hebrew, *Elohim;* Hindoostanee, *Rain;* German, *Gott;* Irish, *Dia;* Italian, *Dio;* Japanese, *Goezur;* Latin, *Deus;* Norwegian, *Gud;* Portuguese, *Deos;* Persian, *Sire;* Peruvian, *Puchecammac;* Spanish, *Dios;* Turkish, *Alah.*

POPULAR ABBREVIATIONS.
SPECIALLY FOR RECORDERS OF COMMANDERIES.

A. C. (*Ante Christum*), Before Christ.

B. C., Before Christ.

A. D. (*Anno Domini*), Year of our Lord.

ÆT., Aged.

A. V., Authorized Version.

D. V. (*Deo Volente*), God willing.

G. M., Grand Master.

IBID. (*Ibidem*), In the same place. ID. (*Idem*), The same.

I. E. (*Id est*), That is.

I. H. S. (*Jesus Hominum Salvator*, or *In Hoc Salus*), Jesus Saviour of men, or In Him is Salvation.

I. N. R. I. (*Iesus Nazarenus Rex Judæorum*), Jesus of Nazareth King of the Jews.

K. T., Knight Templar.

K. M., Knight of Malta.

L. S. (*Locus Sigilli*), Place of the seal.

N. B. (*Nota Bene*), Take notice.

NEM. CON. (*Nemine contradicente*), Unanimously. OB. (*Obiit*), Died.

PRO TEM. (*Pro tempore*), For the time being. PROX. (*Proximo*), Next.

Q. V. (*Quod vide*), Which see.

SC. (*Sculpsit*), Engraved.

ULT. (*Ultimo*), Last.

V. (*Vide*), See.

VIZ. (*Videlicet*), Namely.

ETC. (*Et cetera*), And so forth.

SOME WORDS NOT FULLY UNDERSTOOD

ACRE, *Ack ´-er*, A city of Syria of Crusade interest. ACACIA, *Acay´-shi-a*, An evergreen, thorny plant. ADONAI, *Ay-do ´-nah*, Lord, used where Jehovah occurs. AGNUS DEI, *Ag ´-nus Dee ´-i*, Lamb of God.

AHASUERUS, *Ay-has-yu-ee ´-rus*, King of Persia. ALMONER, *Al ´-mo-ner*, One who distributes alms. ANNO ORDINIS, *An ´-no Or ´-din-is*, Year of the Order. ARTAXERXES, *Ar-tax-erks ´-eez*, King of Persia.

BARABBAS, *Bah-rab´-bas*, One of the Robbers. BEAUCEANT, *Bo´-see-an*, Battle Flag of Templars. BELSHAZZAR, *Bel-shaz´-zar*, King of the Chaldees. BOAZ, *Boh´-az*, A Pillar of the Porch of the Temple. CHAPEAU, *Shah´-po*, A hat.

CLANDESTINE, *Klan-des´-tin*, Hidden, Fraudulent. CONSUMMA- TUM EST, *Kon-sum-mah´-tum est*, It is finished. CRUX ANSA- TA, *Kroox An-sah´-ta*, Cross with a handle.

DARIUS, *Day-ri´-us*, King of Persia.

DIEU LE VEUT, *Dyuh la Voot*, God´s will. DEUS VULT, *Dee´-us Vult*, God´s will.

DIMIT, *Dy-mit´*, To let go.

ECCOSAISE, *Ay´-ko-zayze*, (Rite) Scotch. ECBATANA, *Ec-bat´-ah- nah*. Capital cf the Medes. ELU, *Ayl´-yu*, Elect.

EMERITUS, *Ee´-mer-i-tus*, Out of active service by honorable discharge. EMMANUEL, *Em-man´-u-el*, (Immanuel) God with us.

FRATER, *Fray´-ter*, or *Frah´-ter*, Brother. FRATRES, Brethren.

GAVEL, *Gah´-vel*, The mallet of a Presiding Officer. GETHSEM- ANE, *Geth-sem´-a-nee*, Garden where Jesus was arrested. GOL- GOTHA, *Gol´-go-thah*, A place of a skull.

HEREDOM, *Her´-ee-dom*, Holy House. HOURI, *Hoo´-ree*, Black- eyed nymph. IMPOSTOR, *Im-pos´-tor*, One who deceives. IN- SIGNIA, *In-sig´-ni-ya*, A badge.

JAKIN, *Jah´-kin*, A pillar of the Porch of the Temple. (*Yahkin*.) KABALA, *Kah´-bah-lah*, Jewish Theosophy.

KADOSH KADOSHIM, *Kay-doash´ Kay-doash´-im*, Holy of Holies. KORAN, *Ko-ran´*, Mahometan sacred book.

LAUS DEO, *Laws Dee´-o*, Praise God.

LEGEND *Lej´-end*, A story handed down from ancient times. LIBANUS, *Ly-bah´-nus*, Lebanon.

LUX E TENEBRIS, *Lux ee Ten´-e-bris*, Light out of darkness. MAGDALENE, *Mag-day-lee´-nay*, She of New Testament fame. MAGUS, *May´-jus*, Persian Wise Mau.

MAGI, *May´-ji*, Priest of Magian religion.

MAGIAN, *May´-ji-an*, Believer in religion of the Magi.

MAHER-SHALAL-HASH-BAZ, *Mah´-her-shal´-al-hash-baz*, Make speed to the spoil, hasten the prey.

MELITA, *Mel´-i-ta*, Malta.

NEBUCHADNEZZAR, *Neb-uk-ad-nez´-zar*, King of the Chaldeans. NEBUZARADAN, *Neb-yu-zar-ah´-dan*, General of Nebuchadnezzar. NE VARIETUR, *Nee Var-i´-tur*, To prevent change.

OMNIFIC, *Om-nif´-ik*, All creating. PALESTINE, *Pal´-es-tine*, The Holy Land.

PRO DEO ET PATRIA, *Pro Dee´-o et Pay-tree´-a*, For God and my country. PAX VOBISCUM, *Pax Voh-bis´-kum*, Peace be with you.

PENTATEUCH, *Pent´-ah-tuke*, Five books of Moses. PERSEPOLIS, *Per-sep´-o-lis*, Chief city of Persia.

PRELATE, *Prel´-ate*, Officer of a Commandery, PURSUIVANT, *Pur´-swee-vant*, A messenger.

PYTHAGORAS, *Py-thag´-oh-ras*, A Philosopher of Greece. ROSE CROIX, *Roze Krwah*, Rose Cross.

SATRAP, *Sat´-rap*, A Persian Governor.

SHETHAR-BOZNAI, *Shee´-thar-boz´-nay-i*, Persian nobleman. SHUSHAN, *Shoo´-shan*, A Persian Capital.

TATNAI, *Tat´-nay-i*, A Persian Satrap, or Governor of a province. TETRAGRAMMATON, *Tet-ra gram´ mah-ton*, The concealing number Four. TIRSHATHA, *Tur-shah´-thah*, Persian Governor of Judea.

TURCOPOLIER, *Tur-ko-po´-ly-er*, An ancient Officer of Knights of Malta. VIVA VOCE, *Vy´-vah Voh´-see*, By the living voice.

XERXES, *Zerks´-eez*, King of Persia.

ZERADATHA, *Zer-e-dah´-thah*, Ancient city of Judea.

ZERUBBABEL, *Zer-ub´-bah-bel*, Judean Prince, and Tirshatha.

ZOROASTER, *Zoh-roh-as´-ter*, Founder of Magian religion.

ZARATHRUSTRA, Persian name of Zoroaster.

FRATERNITY MUSIC. OLD HUNDRED. L. M.

HENDON. 7s.

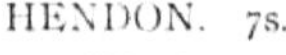

HENDON. 7s.
(SEE PAGE 69.)

1. Lo! the heav'ns its Lord re - ceives, Yet he
2 Lord, tho' part - ed from our sight, Far a -
loves the earth he leaves; 'Tho' re - turn - ing
bove the star - ry height, Grant our hearts may
to his throne, Still he calls man - kind his
thith - er rise, Seek - ing thee a - bove the
own, Still he calls man - kind his own.
skies, Seek - ing thee a - bove the skies.

NEARER, MY GOD, TO THEE.

NEARER, MY GOD, TO THEE.

AULD LANG SYNE.

TO A SKULL.

Part of a poem found beside a skeleton in the Museum of the London Royal College of Surgeons, author unknown. It was published in the Morning Chronicle early in the present century.

Behold this ruin! 'Twas a skull
Once of ethereal spirit full.
This narrow cell was life's retreat;
This space was thought's mysterious seat.
What beauteous visions filled this spot!
What dreams of pleasure long forgot!
Nor hope, nor joy, nor love, nor fear
Has left one trace of record here.
Beneath this mouldering canopy
Once shone the bright and busy eye:
But start not at the dismal void—
If social love that eye employed,
If with no lawless fire it gleamed,
But through the dews of kindness beamed,
That eye shall be forever bright
When stars and sun are sunk in night.
Within this hollow cavern hung
The ready, swift and tuneful tongue:
If falsehood's honey it disdained,
And when it could not praise was chained;
If bold in virtue's cause it spoke—
Yet gentle concord never broke—
 This silent tongue shall plead for thee
When Time reveals Eternity!

TEMPLAR FORMS.

ALTHOUGH the Grand Encampment has not adopted permanent "Templar Forms," the author of SHIBBOLETH suggests the following, to be used until supplanted by Forms adopted by the supreme governing body:

FORM OF PETITION FOR DISPENSATION.

To the Right Eminent Sir —

Grand Commander of Knights Templar of —

The undersigned petitioners respectfully represent that they are Knights Templar in good and regular standing, that they have the prosperity of the Order at heart, and that they desire to promote its influence. In order that a greater opportunity may be afforded them for the same, they are desirous of forming a new Commandery, to be located at —, and to be known as Commandery, No. —. They have nominated and do hereby recommend Sir — to be the first Commander, Sir — to be the first Generalissimo, and Sir — to be the first Captain General of said new Commandery; and they pray for a dispensation empowering them to meet as a regular Commandery at —, in the county of —, there to discharge the duties of Knights Templar in a constitutional manner.

Should the prayer of the petitioners be granted, they promise a strict obedience to the commands of the R. E. Grand Commander, to the statutes and regulations of the Grand Commandery of —, the Constitution and laws of the Grand Encampment, as well as to the usages of the Order.

Dated, −18−

The petition must be signed by at least NINE Knights of the Order, and must be recommended by the Commandery nearest to the place where the new Commandery is to be located.

RECOMMENDATION OF NEAREST COMMANDERY.

Asylum of − Commandery, No. −,

−,18−

At a stated meeting of − Commandery, No. −, held at its Asylum in −, on the − day of −, 18−, the foregoing petition for the formation of a new Commandery at −, in − County, was presented and considered; whereupon it was;

Resolved, That in the opinion of this Commandery good reasons exist for the organization of a Commandery at this time at that place, and the same is hereby recommended by this Commandery. It is hereby certified that said petitioners are Knights Templar of good moral character, and the Sir Knights recommended as officers of said Commandery are capable of conferring correctly the orders of Knighthood.

By order of − Commandery, No. −, [SEAL.], − Eminent Commander.

Attest:

−, Recorder.

CERTIFICATE OF A PAST COMMANDER.

I, —, Past Commander of — Commandery, No. —, do hereby certify that I have examined Sir Knights A B, C D, and E F, the officers recommended in the foregoing petition, in the Rituals of the Orders of the Red Cross, Temple, and Malta, and I find that they are fully capable to confer these Orders correctly.

—, Past Commander.

[SEAL.]

Attest:

—, Recorder.

DISPENSATION FOR NEW COMMANDERY.

IN HOC SIGNO VINCES.

To all whom it may concern:

Know ye, that I, —, Right Eminent Grand Commander of Knights Templar of the State of —, having received a petition from a constitutional number of Fratres, who have been properly vouched for as Knights Templar in good standing, setting forth that, having the prosperity of the Order at heart, they are desirous of establishing a new Commandery at —, under our jurisdiction, and requesting a Dispensation for the same; and,

Whereas, the consent of the nearest Commandery has been granted, and there appears good and sufficient cause for granting the prayer of the said petition, I do, therefore, by virtue of the power in me vested by the Constitution and Laws of the Order, grant this Dispensation, empowering Sir to act as Eminent Commander, Sir — to act as Generalissimo, and Sir — to act as

Captain General of a Commandery to be held under our jurisdiction, at —, in the County of —, by the name — of Commandery, No. —.

And the said Fratres and their associates are authorized to confer the Orders of Knighthood according to the Constitution of
the Order, its customs and usages, and the Rules and Regulations of the Right Eminent Grand Commandery of —, and not
otherwise. This Dispensation shall continue of force until the
next Annual Conclave of the Grand Commandery, unless re-
voked by the Grand Commander.

Given under my hand, and the seal of the Grand Commandery, at —, this — day of — , A. D. 18—, A.

O. 7—.

[SEAL.]

—, Grand Commander.

Attest:

—, Grand Recorder.

CHARTER.

IN HOC SIGNO VINCES

The Right Eminent Grand Commandery of Knights Templar
of the State of —, The Right Eminent —, Grand Commander,

The Very Eminent —, Deputy Grand Commander, The Eminent —, Grand Generalissimo,

The Eminent —, Grand Captain General,

do, by these presents, appoint, authorize and empower our Frater, Sir —, to be the Eminent Commander; our Frater, Sir —, to
be the Generalissimo; and our Frater, Sir —, to be the Captain
General, of a Commandery of Knights Templar, to be, by virtue

hereof, constituted, formed, and held in –, County of –, which Commandery shall be distinguished by the name and style of – Commandery, No. –.; and the said Eminent Fratres, and their successors in office, are hereby respectively authorized and directed, by and with the consent and assistance of a quorum of the members of the said Commandery, duly summoned and present upon such occasion, to elect and install the officers of the said Commandery, as vacancies happen, in manner and form as is or may be prescribed by the Constitution and Regulations of this Grand Commandery.

And further, the said Commandery is hereby invested with full power and authority to assemble upon proper and lawful occasions, to make Knights Templar and to admit members, as also to do and perform all and every such acts and things appertaining to the Order as ought to be done, for the honor and advantage thereof, conforming in all their proceedings to the Constitution and Regulations of this Grand Commandery and the Grand Encampment of the United States; otherwise, this Warrant or Charter, and the powers thereby granted, to cease and be of no further effect.

Given under our hands, and the seal of the Grand Commandery, in the city of –, this – day of –, A. D. 18–, A. O. 7–.

[SEAL.]

–, *Grand Commander,*
–, *Deputy Grand Commander,*
–, *Grand Generalissimo,*
–, *Grand Captain General.*

Attest:
–, *Grand Recorder.*

POWER TO CONSTITUTE A COMMANDERY.

To all whom it may concern:

Whereas, the Right Eminent Grand Commandery of Knights Templar of the State of –, at its last Annual Conclave, empowered by Charter, duly and regularly issued, Sir Knights –, Commander; –, Generalissimo, and –, Captain General, and their successors, to assemble as a regular Commandery, by the name of – Commandery, No. –., and the Constitution of the Order requiring that the same should be duly constituted;

Now, therefore, I, –, Grand Commander of Knights Templar of the State of –, reposing especial trust and confidence in the skill and ability of our Eminent Frater, Sir –, Past Commander of Commandery, No. –, do authorize and empower him, being unable to attend in person, to constitute in form the Sir Knights named in said Charter into a regular Commandery, to be known and hailed by the name aforesaid, and to install the officers elect, agreeably to the Constitution and customs of the Order.

Given under my hand, this – day of –, A. O. 7–.

–, *Grand Commander.*

FORM OF PETITION FOR THE ORDERS.

To the Eminent Commander, Officers and Members of – Commandery, No. –., Knights Templar, stationed at –, State of –:

I hereby declare that I am a Royal Arch Mason in good standing; that I received the degree of Master Mason in – Lodge, No. –., of –, and the degree of R. A. Mason in – Chapter, No. –, of –, and that I am desirous of receiving the Orders conferred in your Commandery.

I further declare that I am a firm believer in the Christian religion.

Should my petition be favorably considered, I promise a cheerful conformity to the rules and usages of the Order and of your Commandery.

This is my — application for the Orders of Knighthood.
If the petitioner has applied previously, he must name the Commandery to which he applied, after this statement.

My age is — Residence — Occupation — Dated at —, —, A. D. 18—.

____

We recommend Companion — to the favorable consideration of the Commandery as a worthy Royal Arch Mason.

____

____

REPORT OF COMMITTEE ON ABOVE PETITION.

The undersigned, a committee appointed to report upon the foregoing petition, respectfully state that they have discharged the trust confided to them, and report —.

____

____

____

—, this — day of —, A. D. 18—.

FORM OF PETITION FOR MEMBERSHIP.

To the Eminent Commander, Officers and Members of — Commandery, No. —., Knights Templar, stationed at —:

I hereby declare that I am a Knight Templar in good standing, and late a member of — Commandery, No. —., stationed at —, as appears by my dimit, herewith presented; and that I am desirous of becoming a member of your Commandery.

My age is — Residence — Occupation —

—, —, A. D. 18—.

____

We recommend Sir — to the favorable consideration of the Commandery as a worthy Knight Templar.

____

____

A committee must report on this petition.

FORM OF DIMIT.

To all whom it may concern:

— Commandery, No. —., Knights Templar, stationed at —, acknowledging the jurisdiction of the Grand Commandery of —, Knights Templar.

NE VARIETUR......

This certifies that Sir —, whose name appears in the margin hereof, is a member of this Commandery in good and regular standing, and having expressed a desire to withdraw his membership, and having paid all his dues to date, is hereby dismissed from the membership of — Commandery, and granted this certificate of the same.

Done at a Stated Conclave of — Commandery, No. —, on the day of —, 18—, A. O. —.

In testimony whereof we have subscribed our names, and affixed the seal of the Commandery.

[SEAL.]

—, Eminent Commander.

—, Recorder.

FORMS FOR TEMPLAR TRIALS.

The important requisites of a Complaint against a Knight Templar are comprehensiveness and clearness. The nature of the offense charged must be clearly defined, and the time, place and circumstances accurately stated, together with the names of the persons who witnessed the commission of the offense. The form of the specification, is important so that there may be no ambiguity. The following is suggested:

COMPLAINT.

To the Eminent Commander, Officers and Members of — Commandery, No. —., K. T:

Sir Knight is hereby charged with immoral and unknightly conduct:

FIRST SPECIFICATION.—That the said Sir —, on the day of — —, 18—, at —, in the county of —, , State of —, did ————.

[Carefully and accurately describe the offense committed.]

in violation of his duty as a Knight Templar, and to the scandal and disgrace of the Order of the Temple.

There should be a Specification for each distinct offense charged, and all should conclude as above. When all the Specifications are set up, then the Complaint may conclude with these words:

It is therefore demanded, that the said Sir — be dealt with according to the law and usages of Templar Knighthood.

———

— this — day of —, 18—.

The Complaint thus drawn will be presented in open Commandery, and if the Commandery receives the same the Eminent Commander will appoint a committee to take testimony, unless the Commandery decides by vote to hear the testimony in open Commandery. These facts must be recorded in the minutes. The full Complaint need not be entered upon the minutes, unless the Commandery so directs, but the nature of the charges should be entered.
The next step is for the Recorder to furnish the accused a complete copy of the Complaint, and its Specifications, and a transcript of the action taken by the Commandery thereon. This form is suggested as the official:

NOTICE TO THE ACCUSED.

Sir —:

Take notice that the foregoing (or the within) charges were preferred against you at a Stated Conclave of — Commandery, No. —, on the — day of, 18—, and that the Commandery decided to hear the testimony in open Commandery (or appointed Sir Knights —, —, —, a committee to take testimony). It (or they) will meet for that purpose on the — day of, 18—, at —, and at — o'clock, — M., at or before which time you are to answer the said charges.

Witness our hand, and the seal of the Commandery, this — day of —, 18—.
[SEAL.]

—, *Recorder*.

These papers may be delivered to the accused in person, or may be mailed to his known address. Great care should be taken to serve these papers in a proper manner. The case should not proceed until service is made, if possible. But if the accused absents himself and purposely avoids service, the delivery of the papers at his home, place of business, or a known place that he resorts, either by personal delivery or through the United States mail, is sufficient.

The papers having been served, the accused will answer, and he may first object to any or all members of the Commission. The Commandery, or Commander, as the procedure maybe, hears his objection, and if the grounds are valid, may select other Fratres to serve as Commissioners.

The accused will answer in his own way, no particular form being of any importance. He may admit and plead extenuating circumstances, or he may deny in part or the whole.

At the time appointed to talk the testimony the accused, if he desires to do so, should appear and first file his answer to the charge, and then proceed to the taking of the testimony. The accused, either by himself or counsel (the latter must be a Knight Templar), has the right to cross-examine witnesses introduced by the opposite party, and also, when the accuser is through with the testimony in support of the charges, to introduce witnesses in leis defense, the opposite party having the right to cross-examine. The accused may, if he prefer, file the answer with the Recorder before the time fixed for taking testimony.

ANSWER OF ACCUSED.

A. B., in person, denies the charges made against him, and every matter and thing contained in the several specifications of the same, and demands trial thereon.

The answer will vary, of course, according to the facts. One specification may be admitted and another denied, or all of them may be admitted, and matters set up in extenuation or excuse. Assuming that the answer is a denial, the next step, unless the witnesses are in attendance at the request of the parties, is to issue, at the request of both parties, process to secure the attendance of the witnesses. The Commandery, or the Committee, should fix the times of meetings, and meet at such times as will secure a prompt investigation of the matter, and at the same time not require such haste as may do injustice to any.

SUMMONS FOR WITNESS.

Sir Knight –:

You are hereby summoned and required to attend as a witness before – Commandery, No. –, at a meeting to be held at its Asylum, on the – day of –, 18–. (or before a Special Committee of – Commandery, No. –, appointed to take testimony, at a meeting to be held by said Committee, at –, on the – day of –, 18–.), then and there to testify as to charges preferred against Sir Knight –, and this you will in no wise omit.

–, Eminent Commander.

– this – day of, 18–.

This may be made to answer for several witnesses by inserting their names, and adding the words "and each of you" after the words "you." This summons can be used, of course, for Knights Templar only. Others attend, if at all, before a Committee, and at their option.

At each meeting of the Commandery (or the Committee) the Recorder of the Commandery, or the Secretary of the Committee, and at its first meeting it should select a Chairman and Secretary, should keep accurate and full minutes of all that transpires on the trial. All motions, exceptions to the competency of testimony, or to the ruling of the Commander or the Committee, should he fully and accurately stated, and the testimony reduced to writing in the exact language of the witness as nearly as may be.

When the testimony is closed on both sides, if taken before a Committee, a report should be made to the Commandery by the Committee. This report should be filed with the Record-

er a sufficient time in advance of a Stated Conclave, to enable him to cause to be summoned all the resident members
of the Commandery to attend at the next Stated Conclave.
The trial may take place at a Special Conclave called by the
Commander for that purpose, but the resident members
must be notified of the time and place, and summoned to
attend.

REPORT OF COMMITTEE.

*To the Eminent Commander, Officers and Members of –
Commandery, No. –, K. T.:*

The Committee appointed to take testimony upon the charges
preferred against Sir Knight A. B. by Sir Knight C. D. has attended to the duty assigned, and submits herewith, as a part of
this report, full minutes of the action of the Committee, as well
as the testimony taken.

– this – day of, 19–.

Committee:

                ————

                ————

                ————

Should the accused admit the charges when served upon him, proof of
such admission or confession will be all that the Committee is required to
have made, and they will make up their minutes and report accordingly.
If the accused fails to appear and answer the charges, after personal service,
the Committee may proceed, after taking proof of such service, to take
proof of the charges.
When this report is submitted to the Commandery, or the testimony is
closed, when taken before the Commandery, the parties concerned may

comment thereon. This, of course, is optional. Before proceeding to vote the accused should retire.

The Commandery then proceeds to consider the matter in the following manner:

FIXING PUNISHMENT.

"Are the charges sustained?" is the first question, and if decided in the affirmative, the Commandery then proceeds, by vote, to fix the punishment. This is done by putting the question:

1st. "Shall the accused be expelled?" If this is decided in the negative;

2d. "Shall the accused be indefinitely suspended?" If this is decided in the negative;

3d. "Shall the accused be definitely suspended?" If this is decided in the affirmative, then, on motion, the time should be fixed by vote; but if decided in the negative;

4th. "Shall the accused be reprimanded?" Which, of course, the other questions having been negatived, will be decided in the affirmative, the charges having been sustained, and this being the lightest punishment which can be inflicted. It would be error for a Commandery to sustain the charges, and then refuse to inflict any punishment.

When the matter is disposed of by the Commandery, the Recorder should at once give notice thereof to the accused.

NOTICE OF JUDGMENT.

To Sir Knight —

Take notice that the foregoing (or the within) is a copy of the action of — Commandery, No. —., upon the charges preferred against you by –, as the same appears of record on the minutes of the Lodge.

–, *Recorder.*

Either party may, within – months from the date of the action of the Commandery, appeal to the Grand Commandery. Notice of the appeal should be given within that time, and the appeal, giving the grounds relied upon, must be filed with the Recorder of the Commandery within – days after notice of appeal, and a copy of the notice and appeal must be forwarded to the Grand Recorder.

NOTICE ON APPEAL.

To, –, Recorder of – Commandery, No. –., Knights Templar:

Take notice, that I shall bring an appeal from the action of said Commandery, on the – day of –, 18–, in passing sentence of – on me, to the R. E. Grand Commandery of the State of –, on the grounds to be stated in my appeal.

A– B–

– this – day of–, 18–.

APPEAL.

To the R. E. Grand Commandery Knights Templar of the State of –:

The undersigned hereby appeals to you from the decision of – Commandery, No. –., made on the – day of –, 18–, in passing sentence of – on him, and he specifies the following as the ground of his appeal:

1st. That – ———.

[State the grounds clearly and truthfully.]

A– B–

this – day of –, 18–.

When the appeal is filed with the Recorder, the Commandery should cause an answer thereto to be prepared, and must furnish the transcript of the proceedings to the Grand Recorder.

ANSWER TO APPEAL.

– Commandery, No. –., answers the appeal of Sir –, and says: That ——————.

–, Eminent Commander.

– this – day of –, 18–. [SEAL]

    Attest:

–, *Recorder.*

The Recorder of the Commandery, in the preparation of a transcript, should be very careful to give fully and exactly all that transpired on the trial, never giving copies unless ordered by the Commandery as to some particular document used, always sending up original papers. The transcript should be made in a plain, legible handwriting, and fastened at top of the paper, and the Recorder should, under the seal of the Commandery, certify to the correctness of the transcript in words like unto the following:

CERTIFICATE TO TRANSCRIPT.

I –, Recorder of – Commandery, No–, Knights Templar, do certify that the foregoing is a full, true, and perfect transcript of all the records and proceedings had by and before said Commandery upon the charges preferred by – against –, as the same appear upon the minutes of said Commandery, and on file in the archives thereof.

In testimony whereof, I hereto subscribe my name and affix the seal of said Commandery this – day of –, A. D. 18–, A. O. 7–.

[SEAL]

–, Recorder.

Recorders should examine with great care the Edicts and Regulations of the Grand Commandery and Grand Encampment upon the subject of trials and appeals, and should strictly conform thereto, varying the foregoing forms as circumstances may require, in order to comply with the requirements of said governing bodies.

APPEAL TO THE GRAND ENCAMPMENT.

In case of a proper appeal to the Grand Encampment, the following form may be substantially adopted:

To the Grand Encampment of Knights Templar of the United States:

The undersigned, your petitioner, respectfully represents that on or about the − day of −, 18−, charges for *immoral and unknightly conduct* (stating the general nature of the charges) were preferred against him by Sir Knight, in − Commandery, No.−, under the jurisdiction of the Grand Commandery of Knights Templar of the State of, and such proceedings were thereupon had in the said − − Commandery; that your petitioner was adjudged by the same Commandery guilty of the offense so charged against him, and was therefore adjudged to (state the penalty imposed). That from such determination and sentence or judgment, your petitioner appealed to the said Grand Commandery, and thereupon such proceedings were had in and by said Grand Commandery; that afterward, and on or about the day − of −, 18−, the said determination and sentence, or judgment, were in *all things affirmed* (state the decision in fact given on the appeal) by the said Grand Commandery; and now your petitioner, feeling himself aggrieved by the action and determination of the said Grand Commandery, in the premises, and being advised that the same is erroneous, appeals therefrom to the Grand Encampment of the United States, and specifies, among other grounds of error therein, the following:

[State the several errors in, and objections to, the proceedings and determination of the Grand Commandery relied upon separately, and numbering them distinctly.]

Your petitioner, therefore, prays that the said Grand Commandery may be required to answer this petition; and that the testimony, proceedings, determination and judgment aforesaid, as well of the said — Commandery, as of said Grand Commandery, may, upon this appeal, be reviewed, and that such sentence and determination, or judgment, may be reversed, modified or amended, as may be agreeable to knightly usage, justice or equity.

———

— this — day of —, 18—.

This appeal should be delivered to the Grand Recorder of the Grand Commandery, and a duplicate thereof delivered to the Grand Recorder of the Grand Encampment. As soon thereafter as practicable, and before the next Triennial Conclave of the Grand Encampment, the Grand Recorder of the Grand Commandery should transmit to the Grand Recorder of the Grand Encampment a transcript of all the testimony, papers, and proceedings in the case which were before the Grand Commandery, together with its action and final determination therein, all duly authenticated under the seal of the Grand Commandery.

PETITION FOR RESTORATION.

To the Eminent Commander, Officers and Members of — Commandery, No. —.:

The undersigned respectfully represents that, on the — day of —, 18—, he was, by the judgment and sentence of said Commandery, expelled (or indefinitely suspended) front the rights and privileges of Knight Templary, and from membership in said Commandery.

For the following reasons (*here state them*) he prays to be restored to the rights and privileges of which he was thus deprived, and promises, if his prayer shall be granted, to conform to the legal conditions of his restoration.

———

— this — day of —, 18—.

THIRD APPENDIX.
RECEPTION OF GRAND VISITORS.

THE following suggestions will aid
Subordinate Commanderies
in receiving Grand Visitors:

THE GRAND MASTER.

The Grand Master is to be received in the Asylum with the highest honors of the Order.

The Grand Master is received by a Committee, and escorted to the quarters of the Eminent Commander.

The Asylum is put in suitable array, Banners unfurled, and the Organist at his post. All Knights in full uniform.

The Lines are formed according to the Tactics of the Jurisdiction, ready to form the Arch of Steel at the proper moment. All Officers in their stations.

The announcement, by the Grand Warder, if present, if not, by one of the Committee attending the Grand Master, is made at the door of the desire of the Grand Master to officially visit the Commandery, whereupon the Warder salutes the Eminent Commander, and says:

W.—Eminent Commander, Most Eminent the Grand Master has arrived, and desires to visit this Commandery officially.

EC.—Sir Knights Generalissimo and Captain General (*these Officers arise, draw and salute*), repair to the quarters of the Most Eminent the Grand Master and escort him hither.

When the Grand Master and suite reach the open door of the Asylum—

W.–THE GRAND MASTER OF TEMPLARS!

Immediately the Organist will play "Hail to the Chief," the Banners will be drooped, and the Officers will salute.

EC.–Form Arch of Steel.
The Grand Master enters, and passes down the avenue, the Generalissimo and Captain General one pace in rear of him, under the Arch of Steel, to the East, where the Eminent Commander receives him, standing on the lowest step of the Dais. He welcomes him in appropriate words, and hands him the Gavel. The Grand Master ascends to the Commander's station, the Eminent Commander, the Generalissimo and Captain General remain standing on the lowest step, and on the floor.
GM.–Sir Knights, *Carry* SWORDS!

He will then make such remarks as he desires, after which the Captain General will dismiss the Lines, and all are seated.

ARRAY OF ASYLUM DURING RECEPTION OF GRAND MASTER.

The following diagrams illustrate formations at two periods of the reception of the Grand Master:

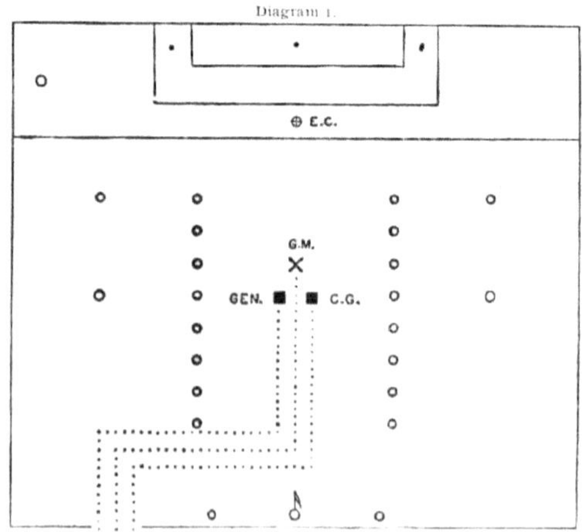

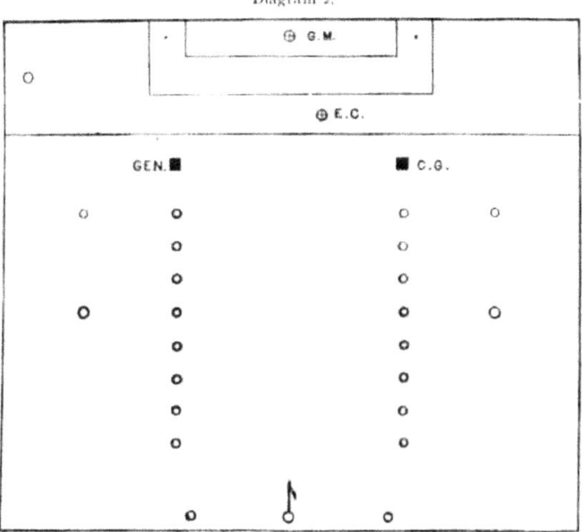

In the first diagram the Grand Master is seen moving towards the East under the Arch of Steel, the Generalissimo and Captain General one step in his rear, and the Eminent Commander awaiting his arrival on the lowest step of the Dais. The Prelate is in his station, standing, and the Senior Warden, the Junior Warden, the Treasurer and Recorder are saluting. The Standard is drooped, and the Senior Warden and the Warder are saluting.

In the second diagram the Grand Master has reached the East, and, Gavel in hand, is about to command "Carry Swords."

THE GRAND COMMANDER.

The Grand Commander is received under the Arch of Steel, Banners drooping, and Officers saluting. Organ plays a March. He is conducted to the Asylum by an escort under command of the Generalissimo. The Grand Commander passes under the

Arch of Steel to the East, where the Eminent Commander receives him, standing on the second step of the Dais, the Captain General on the lowest step.

The Warder will announce–
THE GRAND COMMANDER OF ——— !

The Grand Master and the Grand Commander, and their representatives, are the only visitors that are to be received under the Arch of Steel, or that are to be recognized by any descent from the official positions on the Dais.

THE DEPUTY GRAND MASTER is received like the Grand Master, except the Arch of Steel, the "Hail to the Chief," and the descent from the Dais. The Knights forming the avenue present Swords, the Officers salute, and the organ plays a March.

THE DEPUTY GRAND COMMANDER is received like the Deputy Grand Master, except the organ plays three flourishes.

ALL OTHER GRAND OFFICERS are received with the Officers and members in their regular stations, Officers saluting, members at Present, and Banners drooping. Organ will play one flourish when the visitor enters, and before the Knight escorting him begins his words of introduction. The visitor will stand in the West during the presentation, the Officers and members remaining at Salute and Present until the visitor reaches the East, when the Captain General will bring all to a Carry.

The Eminent Commander will welcome the visitor and assign him a seat.

HINTS TO EMINENT COMMANDERS.

1. Give unremitting attention to the protection of the Ritual, and the Paraphernalia of your Commanderies. The first should never be out of your care, the other should be kept in perfect repair.

2. Be certain that the Sentinel, or Janitor, has everything in readiness for the Conclaves of the Commanderies. The comfort of your Fratres should be an unremitting solicitude. Their attendance will be largely affected by your attention to this hint.

3. See to it that your Fratres are provided with uniforms, but in doing so be not forgetful of the tenderness of many on matters that affect their purses. Persuade, but do not command. Some Grand Commanderies have a rule on this matter of uniforming. Enforce it in love.

4. Do not begin the Opening Ceremonies until you are certain that the Asylum is in proper array, and all necessary arrangements are made.

5. Permit no admissions during the Opening Ceremonies. Allow no conversation, not even whispering, while opening. Such interruptions seriously affect the solemnities.

6. Never begin the Work until you are certain that everything is ready, in place, and in order. Halts to make search for missing paraphernalia are destructive to good Work.

7. Permit no moving about the Asylum, conversation, or comments during the Work. This is of vital importance. Fratres who think they can not refrain from these disturbances should quietly withdraw to the Reception Room, or some other outer apartment. Be certain to make your request for absolute silence before you begin Work.

8. Do not permit military drill during the Work. Form the Escort by arrangements made by the Captain General before the Work begins. Let the chosen Knights so sit that at the low-given command—"Fall in"—they may quietly step to their places, with Swords at a Carry. The formation by counting and facing breaks up all solemnity. And all military commands given should be in subdued tones of voice.

9. This Monitor favors the appearance of none at the D—a, on the First Entrance, but the Eminent Commander, Senior Warden, and Cand. All others seated, and in silence. Asylum in full lights. This is one scene. Second Entrance finds Nine b—d at D—a, and *only* D—a lights burning. This scene is entirely unlike the former,—an important matter of progression. When the PP. re—, the vacancy is symbolized as filled, and he and the two Wardens, with the Nine, make twelve also. The First is a series of Tests by the Chief; the Second is the Filling of the Vacancy caused by

apostasy. If these points are kept in view the Lessons will be most imposing.

10. The author of this Monitor believes that the laying down and taking up the C—s at the Libs is destructive of solemnity. By the method herein suggested there are only two C—s,—one for the Eminent Commander, the other for the Cand. Nothing distracts his attention from the solemn Tests if practiced this way.

RULES OF ORDER.

The following simple rules will be about all that Commanders will find necessary in conducting the business of the Conclaves:

1. On the demand of a member, a motion must be reduced to writing.

2. A motion, when stated by the Commander, can not be withdrawn without the consent of the Commandery.

3. A motion to postpone to an indefinite time is debatable; a motion to postpone to a time definite is not debatable.

4. No amendment beyond an amendment to an amendment can be entertained.

5. A question will be divided on request of a member.

6. A proposition to be referred to a committee *with instructions* is debatable; if *without instructions*, it is not debatable.

7. A Frater voting in the majority may move to reconsider; such a motion is not debatable.

8. When a proposition is reconsidered it is before the Commandery in the exact form it was in at the moment it was voted upon.

9. Before a member is required to vote upon a paper he may require its reading.

10. When the report of a Committee is read, or received, it is the property of the Commandery, and the Committee is discharged without a vote. It may be revived.

11. When the Commander desires the debate to cease he arises, and proceeds to take the necessary steps.

12. A proposition subject to debate is open to debate until the *negative* is put, unless the Commander decides the debate should cease.

The following motions are not allowable in a Conclave of Knights Templar: To lie on the table.

The previous question. To close, or call to rest.

The following questions are not debatable: To read papers.

To grant leave to withdraw a proposition. To postpone to a time definite.

To reconsider a proposition.

To commit without instructions.

A FORM OF DIVINE WORSHIP

FOR THE USE OF KNIGHTS TEMPLAR ON ASCENSION DAY, AND OTHER OCCASIONS.

THE following service is so arranged that, by omitting and adding, it will be applicable to general public occasions, and to Ascension Day.

THE LITURGY.

When the Knights are entering the church or hall they will uncover as they pass the door, and remain standing beside their seats. It is desirable that Swords be not worn; they are so productive of noise and disorder.

Then will be sung, all present participating:

Holy Father, Holy Son,
Holy Spirit, Three in One,
Praise and glory be to thee
Now and through eternity.

P.—The Lord is in his holy temple; let all the earth keep silence before him.

All seated.
Choir will sing some Anthem appropriate to the occasion.

All arise.

P.—What doth the Lord require of thee?

KNIGHTS.—To do justly, love mercy, and walk humbly with our God. P.—O God, thou art my God; early will I seek thee.

KNIGHTS.—My soul thirsteth for thee, my flesh longeth for thee in a dry and thirsty land, where no water is.

P.—My soul followeth hard after thee. KNIGHTS.—Thy right hand upholdeth me. P.—Hear my prayer, O God.
KNIGHTS.—Attend unto my cry.

P.—God be merciful unto us, and bless us. KNIGHTS.—And cause his face to shine upon us. P.—Not unto us, not unto us, O Lord.

KNIGHTS.—But unto thy great name be all the glory.

P.—Blessing, and honor, and glory, and power be unto Him that sitteth upon the throne. KNIGHTS.—And unto the Lamb for ever.

P.—Brethren, let us pray.

The Knights, standing, will unite with the Prelate.

OUR FATHER who art in heaven, hallowed be thy name; thy kingdom come, thy will be done on earth as it is in heaven. Give us this day our daily bread, and forgive us our trespasses as we forgive those who trespass against us. And lead us not into temptation, but deliver us from evil, for thine is the kingdom, and the power, and the glory, for ever and ever. AMEN.

P.—God be merciful unto us, and bless us, and show us the light of His countenance, and be very merciful unto us. AMEN.

Then shall be sung:

THE CORONATION HYMN.

1. All hail the power of Jesus' name,

2. Let angels prostrate fall;

Bring forth the royal diadem,

And crown Him Lord of all!

3. Let every kindred, every tribe,

4. On this terrestrial ball,

To Him all majesty ascribe,

And crown Him Lord of all!

5. O that, with yonder sacred throng,

6. We at His feet might fall

We'll join the everlasting song,

And crown Him Lord of all!

*Or the Te Deum may be sung instead of this Hymn.
Then the Prelate will read:*

THE LESSON.—Ezra vi: 1-15; Psalm li.

If the occasion is Ascension Day—

THE LESSON.—Acts I: 1-9; Mark xvi: 14-20

*If Ascension Day, then will be sung (and the Coronation
Hymn will be omitted in place where given, but the Te Deum maybe sung)—*

KING OF KINGS AND LORD OF LORDS.

1. Look ye, saints, the sight is glorious,

See the man of sorrows now;

From the fight returned victorious,

Every knee to Him shall bow;

Crown Him, crown Him;
Crowns become the Victor's brow.
2. Crown the Savior, angels crown Him;
Rich the trophies Jesus brings;
In the seat of power enthrone Him,
While the heavenly conclave rings;
Crown Him, crown Him;
Crown the Savior King of kings.
3. Hark! those bursts of acclamation;
Hark! those loud triumphant chords;
Jesus takes the highest station;
O what joy the sight affords!
Crown Him, crown Him;
King of kings, and Lord of lords.

If not Ascension Day the above will be omitted, and the Prelate will say, immediately after the Lesson:

P.—Let us pray.

All will kneel.

ALMIGHTY God, our Heavenly Father, King of kings, and Lord of lords, we humbly bow ourselves at thy footstool, and beseech thee to forgive our sins, and blot our transgressions from before thee. Give unto each of us a clean heart, and renew within us a right spirit. Lift upon us the light of thy countenance, and be reconciled to us; and may the words of our mouths, and the meditations of our hearts all be acceptable in thy sight, through Jesus Christ our Lord. AMEN.

God spake these words and said: I am the Lord thy God; thou shalt have no other gods before me. KNIGHTS, OR CHOIR.—

Lord have mercy upon us, and incline our. hearts to keep this law.

P.—Thou shalt not make unto me any graven image, or any likeness of anything that is in heaven above, or that is in the earth beneath, or that is in the water under the earth thou shalt not bow down thyself to them, nor serve them; for I, the Lord thy God, am a jealous God, visiting the iniquity of the fathers upon the children unto the third and fourth generation of them that hate me; and showing mercy unto thousands of them that love me, and keep my commandments.

KNIGHTS.—Lord have mercy upon us, and incline out hearts to keep this law.

P.—Thou shalt not take the name of the Lord thy God in vain; for the Lord will not hold him guiltless that taketh His name in vain.

KNIGHTS.—Lord have mercy upon us, and incline our hearts to keep this law.

P.—Remember the sabbath day to keep it holy. Six days shalt thou labor, and do all thy work; but the seventh day is the sabbath of the Lord thy God; in it thou shalt not do any work, thou nor thy son, nor thy daughter, thy manservant, nor thy maidservant, nor thy cattle, nor the stranger that is within thy gates; for in six days the Lord made heaven and earth, the sea, and all that in them is, and rested the seventh day; wherefore the Lord blessed the sabbath day, and hallowed it.

KNIGHTS.—Lord have mercy upon us, and incline our hearts to keep this law.

P.—Honor thy father and thy mother, that thy days may be long upon the land which the Lord thy God giveth thee.

KNIGHTS.—Lord have mercy upon us, and incline our hearts to keep this law. P.—Thou shalt not kill.

KNIGHTS.—Lord have mercy upon us, and incline our hearts to keep this law. P.—Thou shalt not commit adultery.

KNIGHTS.—Lord have mercy upon us, and incline our hearts to keep this law. P.—Thou shalt not steal.

KNIGHTS.—Lord have mercy upon us, and incline our hearts to keep this law. P.—Thou shalt not bear false witness against thy neighbor.

KNIGHTS.—Lord have mercy upon us, and incline our hearts to keep this law.

P.—Thou shalt not covet thy neighbor's house, thou shalt not covet thy neighbor's wife, nor his manservant, nor his maidservant, nor his ox, nor his ass, nor anything that is thy neighbor's.

KNIGHTS.—Lord have mercy upon us, and incline our hearts to keep this law.

———

Should it be desired to omit the Litany, on Ascension Day, the following prayers shall be said by the Prelate instead:

PRAYERS.

GRANT we beseech thee Almighty Father, that like as we believe thy Son, our Lord Jesus Christ, to have ascended into heaven, so may we now in heart and mind thither ascend, and with Him continually dwell, who liveth and reigneth with thee and the Holy Spirit, world without end AMEN.

O GOD our Father, who hast exalted thy Son to thy right hand, leave us not comfortless we beseech thee, but send down upon us the outpouring of thy Holy Spirit, the Comforter; and in due time, if it so pleases thee, exalt us into thy presence, through Jesus Christ, our Lord and Redeemer. AMEN.

MERCIFUL Father, who on the Pentecostal day didst illuminate the hearts of thy faithful children by sending unto them the light and comfort of thy Holy Spirit, grant us at this time the same spirit, that we may overcome the world and the allurements of the flesh, for Jesus Christ's sake. AMEN.

Should it be desired to omit the Commandments on other occasions than Ascension Day, the Prelate will say the following prayers:

WE THANK THEE Almighty Father, for the memory of thy faithful servants who have fought the good fight, have finished their course, and who kept the faith. Help us to imitate their examples of holy living, and to follow them in all virtuous and godly ways, through Jesus Christ, Emmanuel. AMEN.

MAY it please thee, O God, to guard and govern with thy love our beloved Order of the Temple, its officers and members; its widows and orphans; its sick and afflicted; its poor and distressed. Bestow upon all the spirit of truth, charity, unity and peace; help us to keep our vows, and maintain the faith; endue us with innocency of life, purity of thought and conduct, and firmness of purpose to do the right, through Jesus Christ, our Saviour. AMEN.

FATHER in heaven give to all nations the promised time of peace; build up thy holy temple upon earth, and fill it with thy glory; refresh all hearts with the sweetness of thy grace, and may all done here below soon become pleasing in thy sight, for Jesus Christ's sake. AMEN.

OUR FATHER who art in heaven, hallowed be thy name; thy kingdom come, thy will be done on earth as it is in heaven. Give us this day our daily bread, and forgive us our trespasses, as we forgive those who trespass against us. And lead us not into temptation, but deliver us from evil, for thine is the kingdom, and the power, and the glory, for ever and ever. AMEN.

The Lord's Prayer shall be said at the close of the Ascension Day prayers above.
All will arise.
The Prelate and Knights will repeat together on all occasions—

THE CHRISTIAN'S CREED.

I believe in God, the Father Almighty, maker of heaven and earth; and in Jesus Christ His only Son, our Lord, who was conceived by the Holy Ghost, born of the Virgin Mary, suffered under Pontius Pilate, was crucified, dead and buried; He descended into hell; the third day He arose from the dead, He ascended into heaven, and sitteth on the right hand of God, the Father Almighty; from thence He shall come to judge the quick and the dead.

I believe in the Holy Ghost, the holy catholic church, the communion of saints, the forgiveness' of sin, the resurrection of the body, and the life everlasting. AMEN!

OR THIS:

I believe in God, the Father Almighty; and in Jesus Christ, His only Son, our Lord, who was by the Holy Ghost born of the Virgin Mary, suffered under Pontius Pilate, was crucified and buried; the third day He arose from the dead; He ascended into heaven, and sitteth at the right hand of the Father; from thence He shall come to judge the quick and the dead.

I believe in the Holy Ghost, the Holy Church, the forgiveness of sin, the resurrection of the body, and the life everlasting. AMEN!

If the occasion is Ascension Day, the following will be sung:

> 1. In the cross of Christ I glory,
> Towering o'er the wrecks of time;
> All the light of sacred story,
> Gathers 'round its head sublime.
> 2. When the woes of life o'ertake me,
> Hopes deceive, and fears annoy,
> Never shall the Cross forsake me;
> Lo! it glows with peace and joy.
> 3. Bane and blessing, pain and pleasure,
> By the Cross are sanctified.
> Peace is there, that knows no measure,
> Joys that through all time abide.

If the occasion is other than Ascension Day, the following will be sung:

> 1. From every stormy wind that blows,
> From every swelling tide of woes,
> There is a calm, a sure retreat,
> 'Tis found beneath the Mercy Seat.
> 2. There is a scene where spirits blend;
> Where friends hold fellowship with friends;
> Though sundered far, by faith they meet
> Around one common Mercy Seat.
> 3. There, there on eagle wings we soar,

And sin and sense molest no more,
And heaven comes down our souls to greet,
And glory crowns the Mercy Seat.

Sermon or Address.

DOXOLOGY.

Praise God from whom all blessings flow,
Praise Him all creatures here below,
Praise Him above, ye heavenly host,
Praise Father, Son and Holy Ghost.

BENEDICTION.

The blessing of God Almighty, the Father, the Son, and the Holy Spirit, be amongst you, and remain with you always. AMEN!

RITUAL OF A COMMANDERY
OF SORROW.

GRAND COMMANDERIES often desire to hold imposing Memorial Services in honor of their distinguished dead. Subordinate Commanderies have the sane privilege. When the Ceremonials are pathetic and tender, the results are most beneficial.

The ceremonies are public, and may be held in the Asylum, or in a public hall.

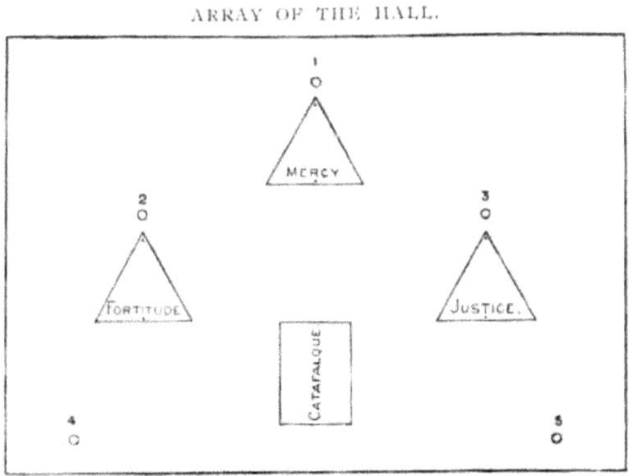

This diagram represents an elevated stage. 1, Commander; 2, Generalissimo; 3, Captain General; 4, Prelate; 5, Commander of the deceased Knight's commandery.

The three triangular tables should be 30 inches high, and have sides 15 inches long. They should each have a valance reaching to the floor. On each table should be three tall tapers, all burning.

The Catafalque is properly shaped thus (end view):

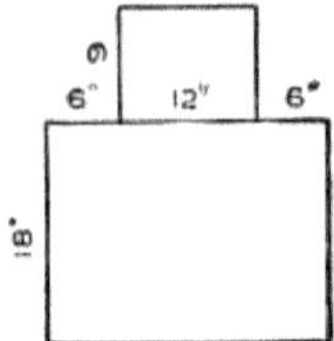

It should be 32 inches long at the base, and the top part 24 inches long. This gives a terrace 6 inches wide all around, on which should be 12 lighted tapers, four on the front, and four on each side. On the top of the Catafalque a white urn may be placed, and all properly draped, and decked with white flowers.

A large bell, best made out of a bar of steel, is suspended near the chair of the commander, who will toll the same at the proper time.

A floral crown, and a floral cross should be prepared, and placed convenient to the proper officers. A floral wreath should be wound around a sword, and placed near the chair of the Captain General.

The Officers should be in full Templar costume, and the Prelate in regulation robes. If possible, all the knights should be in full Templar costume.

The music should be effectively rendered, and should be solemn and pathetic.

The ceremonials should be conducted in a slow and measured manner, solemnity and tenderness being the chief characteristics.

The officers enter in procession, and when they have taken their stations the ceremonies will begin.

THE CEREMONIES.

Choir sings "Rock of Ages," or other appropriate music:

COMMANDER.—Sir Knights, a Pilgrim Warrior, a soldier of the Cross, a Companion beloved, has been summoned hence. He has obeyed the summons and laid aside his armor. There is a vacancy in the Grand Commandery of —;a vacant chair in our council chamber. A taper has been extinguished here, to be re-lighted up yonder.

When the Commander says, "extinguished here," he will pause, and extinguish the taper at the apex of his triangular table. When he says, "to be relighted up yonder," he will relight the taper.

Beloved, we have gathered together to honor the memory of a Companion in arms, Sir Knight —; to tender condolence to the bereaved, and to crave permission to mingle our tears with theirs. The occasion is stricken with sorrow, but its poignancy is mollified by the preciousness of the hope of that other life, where tears and sorrows are unknown. In the midst of life we are in death; but unto whom shall we go for succor but unto Him who tempers the wind to the shorn lamb. Excellent Prelate, read unto us from the Father's will.

FIRST LESSON.

Prelate reads Job xiv: 1, 2, 5-14; 1 Corinthians xv: 12-23.

P.—Man that is born of a woman is of few days, and full of trouble. He cometh forth like a flower, and is cut down; he fleeth also as a shadow, and continueth not. Seeing his days are determined, the number of his months are with thee, thou hast appointed his bounds that he can not pass, turn from him that he may rest till he shall accomplish, as an hireling, his day. For there is hope of a tree if it be cut down that it will sprout again, and that the tender branches thereof will not cease. Though the root wax old in the earth, and the stock thereof die in the ground, yet through the scent of water it will bud and bring forth boughs like a plant.

But man dieth and wasteth away; yea, man giveth up the ghost, and where is he? As the waters fail from the sea and the flood decayeth and drieth up, so man lieth down and riseth not; till the heavens be no more they shall not awake nor be raised out of their sleep.If a man die shall he live again? All the days of my appointed time will I wait, till my change come. Thou shalt call, and I will answer thee.

But if there be no resurrection of the dead, then is Christ not risen. And if Christ be not risen, then is your preaching vain, and your faith is also vain. * * * For if the dead rise not, then is not Christ raised; and if Christ is not raised, your faith is vain; ye are yet in your sins. * * * If in this life only we have hope in Christ, we are of all men most miserable.

But now is Christ risen from the dead, and become the first fruits of them that slept. For since by man came death, by man came also the resurrection of the dead. For as in Adam all die, even so in Christ shall all be made alive. But every man in his order; Christ the first fruits, afterward they that are Christ's at his coming.

Brethren, let us pray.

PRAYERS.

ALMIGHTY and most Merciful Father, who has commended us to love one another as thy children, send down upon us at this time the dew of thy heavenly grace; pardon all our transgressions; renew within us right spirits, and refresh us with the sweetness of thy love; give unto us faith and hope so that this, our sorrow, may conduce to our eternal happiness. Look with compassion upon these bereaved ones, and pour into their bleeding hearts the consolations of thy grace; and may they have part and lot with all thy saints, through Jesus Christ, our Lord. AMEN.

COMMAND thy blessing, O God, to abide with all who are sick or afflicted; with the widow and the orphan; with the dying and the convalescent; with the poor and the distressed. Bestow upon all the spirit of thy grace, and help us to bear each other's burdens, so that having lived together in love here, we may, through the merits of our once crucified, but now risen and exalted Redeemer, ascend unto that peace that remaineth to the people of God, and forever unite in singing the praises of redeeming love. And to thy great and matchless name shall be all the praise and glory, through Jesus Christ, Emmanuel. AMEN.

The grace of our Lord, Jesus Christ, and the love of God, and the fellowship of the Holy Ghost be with us all evermore. AMEN.

CHOIR.–

ASLEEP IN JESUS.

TUNE, *Zephyr.*

1. Asleep in Jesus! blessed sleep!
From which none ever wake to weep;
A calm and undisturbed repose.
Unbroken by the last of foes.

2. Asleep in Jesus! O how sweet
To be for such a slumber meet;
With holy confidence to sing
That death bath lost its venomed sting.

3. Asleep in Jesus! O for me
May such a blissful refuge be;
Securely shall my ashes lie,
And wait the summons from on high.

4. Asleep in Jesus! far from thee
Thy kindred and their graves may be;
But there is still a blessed sleep
From which none ever wake to weep.

While the last verse is being sung the Commander will toll the Bell, and the hall lights will be slowly lowered, until a dim light pervades.

THE CEREMONIES.

The Captain General will arise with the wreathed sword in hand.

CG.–In the hands of our deceased Companion this sword was endowed with three inestimable qualities–Justice, Fortitude and Mercy. Whenever he grasped this glittering sword, his hand first laid hold upon the cross, (*holding cross of sword upwards*), and before he drew it from its scabbard he was well assured of the JUSTICE of his cause.

I lay his Sword, wreathed with emblems of our affection, on this Triangle dedicated to JUSTICE.

The Captain General remains standing, and after a pause the Generalissimo rises.

G. (*With floral Cross in hand*)–Our Companion delighted to wear upon his breast this emblem of the Christian Faith. He could exclaim with the apostle, "God forbid that I should glory save in the cross of our Lord, Jesus Christ." May this (*raising the Cross*) be the token to admit him where the wicked cease from troubling, and the weary are at rest.

To the memory of his Christian fidelity, courage and constancy, I lay this emblem on the Triangle dedicated to FORTITUDE.

The Generalissimo remains standing. A pause, then the Commander rises.

C. (*With floral Crown in hand*)–" Be thou faithful unto death and I will give thee a crown of life." Because our Companion was faithful do we hope that a crown awaited him in that "house not made with hands, eternal in the heavens." This emblem of that hope, (raising floral Crown) I now deposit on the Triangle dedicated to MERCY.

Excellent Prelate, lead our Devotions. P.—Beloved, let us kneel in prayer.

The Choir will sing in soft, low voices:

> 1. Just as I am, without one plea,
> But that thy blood was shed for me,
> And that thou bidst me come to thee,
> O Lamb of God I come.
>
> 2. Just as I am, thou wilt receive,
> Wilt welcome, pardon, cleanse, relieve;
> Because thy promise I believe,
> O Lamb of God I come.
>
> 3. Just as I am, thy love unknown,
> Hath broken every barrier down;
> Now, to be thine, yea, thine alone,
> O Lamb of God I come.

The Prelate will then offer the following, all still kneeling:

PRAYER.

HEAVENLY Father, in whose holy sight centuries are but as days, look down upon these bowed, weary pilgrims who are traveling through this vale of tears, and soften their afflictions with the consolations of thy Holy Spirit, the Comforter. Accept the homage we bring, and permit us to come unto thee, O Lamb of God, our Redeemer, so that there may be revived in each heart

the hope of eternal felicity, through Jesus Christ, our Saviour.
AMEN.

As the word Amen is pronounced the lights of the hall will be flashed up, and all will be seated.

THE CHANT OF MOURNING.

The Choir will then chant the following selection of Scripture:

In the day when the keepers of the house shall tremble, and the strong men shall bow themselves and the grinders cease because they are few, and those that look out of the windows be darkened.

And the doors shall be shut in the streets, when the sound of the grinding is low, and he shall rise up at the voice of the bird, and all the daughters of music shall be brought low;

Also when they shall be afraid of that which is high, and fears shall be in the way, and the almond tree shall flourish, and the grasshopper shall be a burden, and desire shall fail; because man goeth to his long home, and the mourners go about the streets;

Or ever the silver cord be loosed, or the golden bowl be broken, or the pitcher be broken at the fountain, or the wheel broken at the cistern.

Then shall the dust return to the earth as it was; and the spirit return unto God who gave it.

ADDRESS BY THE COMMANDER.

C.–Sir Knights, each bereavement severs a sordid cord that binds us to this lower life, and stretches a golden one from earth to heaven. These severings command a halt, send us into the solitude of reflection, and enquire if we are able to answer the necessary questions, and wash our hands in innocency, in token of our sincerity.

Brethren, the memory of him who falls in a just cause is forever blessed. That just cause to us means defense of holy religion, feeding the hungry, clothing the naked, and binding up the wounds of the afflicted. It was in such a cause our Brother was engaged when he fell, and his memory shall forever flourish in immortal green. Though he now sleeps the long, undisturbed repose of death, his virtues are fresh, and live in our hearts. In the darkness of the tomb his ashes but await the summons of the resurrection, and his glorified spirit, we trust, is now engaged in hymning the praises of redeeming love.

Let us, therefore, having hope in God, lay aside the drapery of our mourning, and ascending out of the darkness of our grief into the light of the promises of our Great Captain, perform this last duty to the memory of our friend.

Companion Commander of – Commandery, on whose rolls the name of our Frater was inscribed, receive the instructions of this Grand Commandery.

The Commander arises, and meets the Grand Commander in middle of stage.

Here on this scroll is inscribed the name, age and advancements of our beloved Frater, now deceased. Bear it to your Asylum, and there deposit it in the archives, in constant and perpetual memorial.

C.–Right Eminent Sir, I accept this memorial scroll in the name of — Commandery. It shall be sacredly deposited in the archives.

Both remain, facing the audience, when the Prelate will say:

P.–"I heard a voice from heaven saying unto me, WRITE: from henceforth blessed are the dead who die in the Lord; even so saith the spirit, for they rest from their labors."

The Commanders go to their stations, and all are seated except Grand Commander.

C.–Sir Knights, these ceremonies have refreshed us, comforted our hearts, and strengthened our faith. Let us all henceforth so let our light shine that the world seeing, our good works may glorify our Father who art in heaven. May we so live that when we die our friends will deem it a pleasant duty to bestrew our graves with flowers, and thereby cherish the memory of our virtues.

THE EULOGIUM.

The Eulogium will then be pronounced by the orator selected
After the Eulogium the Choir will sing, and the congregation will arise and join.

THE CONSOLATORY.

1. Forever with the Lord!
Amen! so let it be;
Life from the dead is in that word,
'Tis immortality.

2. Here in the body pent,
Absent from thee I roam,
Yet nightly pitch my moving tent
A day's march nearer home.

3. Forever with the Lord!
Father, if 'tis thy will,
The promise of that faithful word
E'en here to me fulfill.

The Excellent Prelate will then pronounce the:

BENEDICTION.

The grace of the Lord, Jesus Christ, and the love of God, and the communion of the Holy Ghost be with you all. AMEN.

THE CHRISTMAS OBSERVANCE.

THE Grand Encampment, at its Triennial Conclave, Denver, 1892, gave its sanction to the Christmas Toast and Response, which had been inaugurated by Sir Stephen Berry, of Portland, Maine, and it made him Chairman of the Committee, *ad vitam!* He is charged with the duty of annually preparing the sentiment.

———

On Christmas Day the Knights will assemble in their Asylum one hour before the official Hour of Observance, without uniforms. The hours are:

Eastern Time, 12 noon.　　*Central Time*, 11 o'clock.
Western Time, 10 o'clock.　　*Pacific Time*, 9 o'clock.

The Triangle will be placed in position, on which will be twelve goblets, also one on the pedestal of the Commander. Glasses will be provided for all the Templars present.

Allowing a sufficient time in which to perform the following exercises before the Official Hour arrives, the Commander, Prelate and Recorder will take their stations, the Knights will be seated as usual, and the Commander will sound his gavel.

HARK, THE HERALD! 7s.

1. Hark the herald! angels sing
Glory to the new born king;
Peace on earth, and mercy mild,
God and sinners reconciled.

2. See He lays his glory by;
Born that man no more may die,
Born to raise the sons of earth;
Born to give them second birth!

3. Hail the holy Prince of peace!
Hail, the Son of righteousness!
Light and life to all He brings,
Risen with healing in His wings!

More elaborate Music may be used if desired by the participants.

EC.—Excellent Prelate, read us the old, old story.

Prelate reads Isaiah xi: I-5; Matthew is 18; Luke ii: 4, 18-14.

P.—And there shall come forth a rod out of the stem of Jesse, and a branch shall grow out of his roots. And the spirit of the Lord shall rest upon him, the spirit of wisdom and understanding, the spirit of counsel and might, the spirit of knowledge and the fear of the Lord; and shall make of him quick understanding in the fear of the Lord; and he shall not judge after the sight of his eyes, neither reprove after the hearing of his ears.

With righteousness shall he judge the poor, and reprove with equity for the meek of the earth; and he shall smite the earth with the rod of his mouth, and with the breath of his lips shall he slay the wicked. And righteousness shall be the girdle of his loins, and faithfulness the girdle of his reins.

***

Now the birth of Jesus Christ was on this wise: when as his mother Mary was espoused to Joseph, before they came together, she was found with child of the Holy Ghost. Then Joseph her husband, being a just man, and not willing to publicly expose her, was minded to put her away privily.

But while he thought on these things, behold, the angel of the Lord appeared unto him in a dream, saying, Joseph, son of David, fear not to take unto thee Mary thy wife; for that which is conceived in her is of the Holy Ghost. And she shall bring forth a son, and thou shalt call his name JESUS; for he shall save his people from their sins.

Now all this came to pass, that it might be fulfilled which was spoken of the Lord by the prophet, saying, Behold a virgin shall be with child, and shall bring forth a son, and they shall call his name Emmanuel, which being interpreted is, God with us.

****

And Joseph went up from Galilee, out of the city of Nazareth, into Judea, unto the city of David, which is called Bethlehem.

And lo, an angel of the Lord came upon them, and the glory of the Lord shone round about them; and they were sore afraid. And the angel said unto them, fear not: for behold, I bring you good tidings of great joy, which shall be to all people. For unto you is born this day in the city of David a Saviour, which is Christ the Lord. * * * And suddenly there was with the angel a multitude of the heavenly host praising God, and saying,

CHOIR.—Glory to God in the highest, and on earth peace, good will among men.

Then shall be sung in an adjacent room, but which singing must be quite distinct in the Asylum, a solo:

LO! A STAR, YE SAGES HOARY.

1. Lo! a star, ye sages hoary;
Lo! a wondrous star above!
He is born, the King of glory,
He, our wondrous star of love.

2. Lord of life, Redeemer, Master,
Loud the shepherd's welcome rolls,
He is born, the people's shepherd,
Aye, the shepherd of our souls.

CHOIR—(*Arranged as an Anthem.*)

Praise God from whom all blessings flow;
Praise Him all creatures here below;
Praise Him above, ye heavenly host,
Praise Father, Son and Holy Ghost.

If sung in long measure merely, all Templars present should join.

EC.–Sir Knights, on this joyous day we commemorate the Birth of JESUS of Nazareth, Emmanuel, author of our salvation, and the Great Captain under whose Banner all of us have enlisted.

On this day 189— years ago, there was born in Bethlehem of Judea, one who laid aside the god-head, and assumed mortal flesh; one whose glory, worth and grace no language can express; one who was horn that our lives might be purified, and who died that our souls might be redeemed from the penalty of sin.

Let us, as true Soldiers of the Cross, strive to profit by the birth, life, death, resurrection and ascension of that divine Master, and remain His faithful soldiers unto death. Seeking strength to continue that struggle let us now accompany our Excellent Prelate to the throne of the heavenly grace. Excellent Prelate, lead our devotions.

All arise, then kneel on the right knee, and how heads.
The Excellent Prelate will offer the following:

PRAYER.

ALMIGHTY and most merciful Father, remember us with pity, we beseech thee, and blot out the multitude of our transgressions, for thy beloved son's sake. And may the words of our mouths, and the meditations of our hearts be acceptable in thy sight, through Jesus Christ, our Lord.
ALL.–AMEN!

FATHER in heaven command thy blessing to rest upon all true Knights of the Temple wherever dispersed; bestow upon them a spirit of Truth, Justice, Courage, Constancy, Faith and Humility, and make of them valiant defenders of thy holy religion. Teach them to feed the hungry, clothe the naked, and bind up the wounds of the afflicted, for Jesus' sake.

ALL.–AMEN!

O LORD command thy benediction to rest upon our Grand Master. Help him to rule over us in love, and with an eye single to thy glory. Save him from error, prejudice and pride; and while giving him firmness of purpose to do right, help him to know the right, for Christ's sake.

ALL.–AMEN!

FATHER, let thy choicest blessings be with the President of the United States, and upon all in authority over us. Endue them with wisdom from on high, and may it be their chiefest joy to labor for thy glory, and the good of the people for whom they legislate, and over whom they rule. Which we ask in the name of Jesus, Emmanuel.

ALL.–AMEN!

If there are any minutes to spare, conversation and congratulations will now occur, while twelve Knights are being selected to form around the Triangle. At exactly five minutes before the Official Hour the Eminent Commander will sound his gavel, when all will he seated.

The Eminent Commander will then say:

EC.–Let the chosen twelve form around the Triangle. (*Done*) .

Let the water be poured into the goblets on the Triangle, and on the Pedestal. (*Done*).

Let every Knight be furnished with a prepared goblet. (*Done*)

Thus prepared, there will be silence until two minutes before the Hour. This Monitor does not suggest what the fluid shall be, save at the Triangle, and on the Commander's pedestal. Some will prefer wine, some water. The writer simply suggests to his Fratres that even a semblance of intemperance should not be witnessed within an Asylum of Knights Templar. Just two minutes before the hour:

THE TOAST.

EC.–Sir Knights, arise! Sir Knight Recorder, read the sentiment.

The Recorder will read the sentiment, clear and loud.

EC.–(*On the first stroke of the Hour.*) To our Grand Master! Drink.

The Knights repeat," To our Grand Master," and drink.

EC.–Sir Knight Recorder, read Grand Master' s Response.

The Recorder will read the Response in a clear, loud voice.

OTHER TOASTS.

The Eminent Commander will then offer the following Toasts, which will be drank in the same manner as that to the Grand Master.

1. To the Grand Commander, Knights Templar, of —
2. To all Knights Templar wherever dispersed.
3. To all Knights Templar who have shed their blood in defense of liberty and Christianity. (*Silence, and heads bowed; no drinking*).
4. To the Grand Master of Masons in —
5. To the Grand High Priest of the Royal Arch Chapter of —

IN MEMORIAM.

EC.—Let us recall the virtues of the Fratres of our own jurisdiction who have joined the silent majority.

The Knights at the Triangle will lay their goblets on the Triangle.

EC.—In memory of the dead of this jurisdiction during the year 189—

The Knights at the Triangle will drop on the right knee, all the Knights will bow their heads, and then will be sung, in soft tones, by the Choir:

> Nearer, my God to thee
> Nearer to thee!
> E'en though it be a cross
> That raiseth me;
> Still all my song shall be,
> Nearer, my God to thee,
> Nearer to thee!

EC.—Sir Knights, arise. We have been refreshed by these hallowed memories, now let us receive the benediction of our Excellent Prelate.

BENEDICTION.

P.—May the Lord bless thee and keep thee; may the Lord make His face to shine upon thee and be gracious unto thee; may the Lord lift up His countenance upon thee, and give thee peace.

———

END OF THE OBSERVANCE.

FORM OF RECORDER'S MINUTES.

ASYLUM OF – COMMANDERY, No. –., K. T.

–, January 1, 189–, A. O. 77–.

– Commandery, No–, met in Stated (or * Called) Conclave, in its Asylum, the – day of–, 189–, and a Commandery of Knights Templar was opened in due form, with,

OFFICERS:

Eminent Sir –, Commander.

Sir –, Generalissimo.

Sir –, Captain General.

Sir –, Prelate.

Sir –, Senior Warden.

Sir –, Junior Warden.

Sir –, Treasurer.

Sir –, Recorder.

Sir –, Standard Bearer.

Sir –, Sword Bearer.

Sir –, Sentinel.

Members–Sirs A. B., D. E., etc.

Visitors–Sir X. Y., Mary Commandery, No. 4, Philadelphia, etc.

It was announced that the Right Eminent Grand Commander had arrived, and desired to visit the Commandery officially. Whereupon, the Arch of Steel was formed, and the distinguished visitor was received with the honors befitting his rank.

After a few pleasant remarks by the Right Eminent Grand Commander, the Lines were dismissed, and the business of the Commandery continued.

Minutes of the preceding Conclave were read, and approved as correct.

Petition from Companion —, member of — Lodge, No. —, and of, Hamilton Chapter, No. —, for the Orders of Knighthood, was read, and referred to the following:

Committee—Sirs A. B. C., X. Y. Z., and G. W. P.

The following bills, approved by the Finance Committee, were read and ordered paid, viz.: [insert bills.]

The committee on the petition of Companion — reported, whereupon the ballot was spread, and he was declared duly elected to receive the Orders of Knighthood.

The committee on the petition of Sir —, for affiliation, reported, whereupon the ballot was spread, and he was declared rejected.

Sir Knight — offered the following, which was adopted:

Resolved, That, etc. [insert resolution.]

The business of the Commandery was then suspended, and a:

COUNCIL OF THE RED CROSS

was opened, the officers assuming the titles thereof.

Companions A. B. C., G. F. S. and H. Y. T., who had been duly elected, were in waiting, and, there being no objection, were introduced and created and constituted Companions of the Illustrious Order of the Red Cross.

The Council was then closed, and the business of the Commandery was resumed.

Sir Knight — petitioned for a demit, and he being clear of the books, the same was granted. The Commandery was then closed in due form.

After closing the Commandery, the Right Eminent Grand Commander was escorted by the Fratres, without uniform, to the banquet hall.

[Make the record of this as full as may be desired.]

———————

Commander.

———————

Recorder.

———————

When the Minutes are approved they should be signed at once by the Commander and Recorder.

The Minutes should not record the nature of the report of a Committee on Petitions. The above form is the correct one.

The Records should he carefully paragraphed, written in a clear style of writing, as well as composition. Many Recorders crowd the records, thus making them indistinct.

Use a Record Book that has a ruled margin, and give marginal notes.

Prompt Recorders always have the "Rough Minutes" ready at the close of each Conclave. They can then be corrected by those who participated. The minutes are read to the next Conclave as information.

Reports of Treasurer and Recorder are spread on the Minutes as *information*, and should not be voted upon, and never inserted as "adopted."

ASYLUM, AND PRELATE'S HALL.

THIS plate illustrates how a Commandery that has only one large apartment can utilize the same for the Asylum and Prelate's Hall, during the conferring of the Order of the Temple.

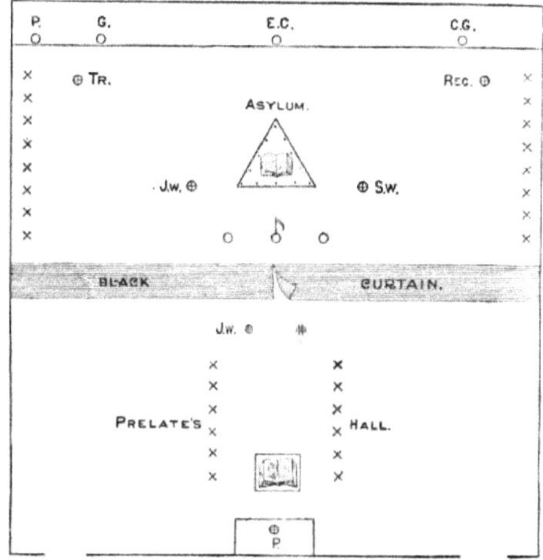

The same arrangement is available in the Red Cross. The Asylum becomes the Audience Chamber, and the Prelate's Hall becomes the Council Chamber. Of course the Standard Bearer removes his chair to allow the entrance of the Candidate.

As a rule this arrangement is to be preferred except in Temples where there is a large Prelate's Hall separate from the Asylum.

HINTS ON TEMPLAR BANQUETS.

THE social features of the assemblies of the Knights of the Temple will not be neglected by prudent Commanders. A reception and Banquet, which include the ladies, and given at least annually, is one of the very best investments a Commandery can make.

The management of the Reception need not be commented upon, but as a Templar Banquet is somewhat unique, hints may be of value to many Commanders.

De *not* form a Passion Cross with the tables. That cross is a sacred symbol in the Order of the Temple, and is not associated with the hilarity usual to a Banquet. The following form is suggested. It is very desirable that the banqueters sit as compactly as possible, and close up to the Commander, so as to be easily governed at proper intervals.

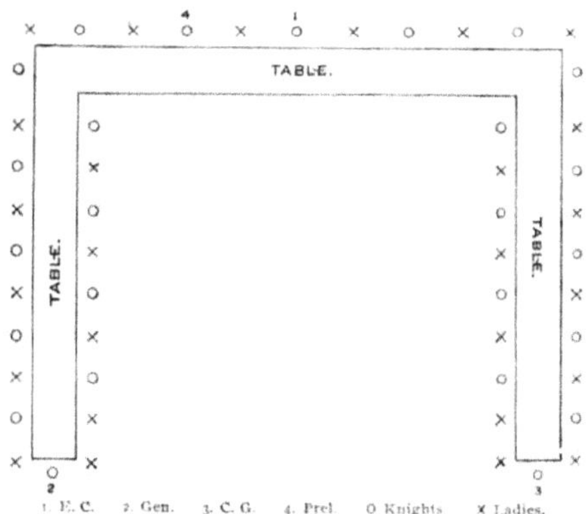

This form allows the waiters easy access, and permits all to see the Commander, or Toastmaster.

The placing of the speakers at various points at the table is helpful to the listeners. It will be wise to seat the speakers in the places selected before the doors are thrown open.

Not more than five distinct courses, nor more than five speakers, beginning at nine and closing not later than midnight, will make the entertainment agreeable to most.

A few crisp remarks by the Commander, in introducing each speaker, may add to the brilliancy of the toast and the response. Do not he personal unless you know your speaker.

Never permit smoking when ladies are present.

Table of Contents

MASONICA

Publishers of the Ancient Craft